A PILG

MW01492366

RE
ST

BYRON YAWN   RYAN HASKINS   JON MOFFITT   JEREMY LITTS

Theocast, Inc.
P.O. Box 592
Nolensville, TN 37135
(615) 212-9212
www.theocast.org

ISBN-10: 0-692-18290-X
ISBN-13: 978-0-692-18290-1

To the members and elders of Community.
Thank you for your uncompromising and
unrelenting commitment to the true Gospel.

CONTENTS

IN THE BEGINNING...

Theocast happened for one basic reason. A friend and church member was sitting with the staff one evening listening to us work through some nuanced theological topic. The conversation was—as always—enlightening on numbers of levels. Once it winded down and we were exiting the space, our friend said, "There has to be a way the rest of us can be exposed to this level of conversation. This isn't fair. That was amazing! You guys don't need to keep this to yourself." The four of us—Jon, Jeremy, Ryan and Byron—were only doing what we do. We had not considered that others might enjoy being invited here. Truth is, our conversations are precious to us personally. We've sat for hours countless times talking about Jesus. Sometimes we end in tears. Sometimes our voices are raised. Always there is laughter.

Always there are more questions raised than answered. Our office space is set up with a view to creativity and thoughtfulness. There's this central area with chairs and a floor to ceiling custom board for sharing ideas. This space is a vortex for these exchanges. Rarely do we pass through it without being pulled into the transcendent. "Hey, can I ask you a question…" and suddenly all our minds engage. Theocast is an invitation for the "layman" to join the conversation; to listen to flawed but sincere human beings with enough knowledge to be dangerous, wrestle through the most profound truths known to man.

Every week the four of us lend our voices to a conversation about a given topic. One of the secrets of our podcast's success (relative as it is) is the chemistry and love that exists among the four of us. We're dear friends and it shows. This allows the voices and perspectives of each to shape the conversation. The more of us there are sitting around looking at Jesus, the more things we'll be able to see than if it was just one of us. I'm always astounded at what the other guys see that I didn't. Always. I'm always grateful for their voices. We've each etched out our own space on the podcast. We all respect each other's space. Our listeners have tuned their ears to the four of us. This book is written with those voices in mind. As you read you'll hear each one of us in the same way you would around our table in studio. The book moves like one of our shows does—from voice to voice. You'll see this as you move from chapter to chapter. So if you don't listen to our podcast and wonder why each chapter sounds so, now you know.

As far as style is concerned, there's one other thing you'll notice. At certain points, words and concepts are used without any background or footnotes. In this sense the writing is placed a little higher up on the shelf. You have to reach to get it. This is intentional. We need to stretch ourselves theologically in order to catch the vision of the Reformers and what they were saying. As we write we are not thinking: How can I lower this idea down to the reader? We are thinking: How can I elevate the reader up to this idea? There is a difference. The former follows the contemporary trend of ease in thinking, also known as convenience. The latter follows a more rigorous manner of learning, also known as thinking. You might need to Google some things you come across (or maybe not). That's a good thing. When I was in seminary I developed a research habit. As I sat and listened to each professor I made note of every concept, resource, author, or controversy I was unfamiliar with. In the back of each syllabus I had three or four blank pieces of paper where I wrote them all down. Immediately following class every day I'd descend to the library and start filling in the blanks of my understanding. I would fall down these rabbit holes of discovery. That was one of the more beneficial exercises of my education. Basically, we're inviting you to the same experience. If it does not immediately register, go searching for it. You will not regret it.

INTRODUCTION

Pilgrim's Guide to Rest is what happens when friends get around to putting their hearts and souls down in words. That's this book. We dipped out our deepest convictions and vision for the Church, and spread them out across these several humble chapters. We have no idea how they'll be received. (OK, maybe a slight idea.) There's always a risk involved in putting yourself out there as we have. There's always the concern that all the "clarity" was only in our heads. The space between writing and reception is a breeding ground for all sorts of fears: rejection, misunderstanding, confusion, or correction. Our concerns are heightened in that we're deconstructing concepts and constructs that have been largely assumed by people in the Church for generations. This has the potential to invoke an intense reaction as people sense the foundation shifting beneath them. It's happened before—in our own church as a matter of fact. This reaction is understandable. At certain times these sorts of responses were the result of poor delivery on our part. For certain, we can always say things better. As a result, we've adjusted our language and delivery along the way. But, no amount of "wordsmithing" can alleviate the tension created when basic assumptions are challenged by new voices. People will have to wade through these waters themselves and come to their own conclusions.

Robert Frost has a poem entitled the *West-Running Brook*. It's an analogy drawn from a brook on his farm intended to explain his effect as a poet within the world of poetry. Frost's poetry was like a brook on his farm that flowed west away from the ocean when every other brook flowed east towards it as nature dictated. That's how Frost saw his style; it was a challenge to convention. As Frost wrote, "Here we, in our impatience of the steps, get back to the beginning of beginnings, the stream of everything that runs away." Getting back to beginnings and foundations means going against traditional tides and challenging conventional thinking. In so doing you are not moving away from the truth, but toward it. It's a painful resistance to go upstream, but clarity is that way. It's important to understand that *Theocast* flows in an opposite direction set against popular tides. This is by design. We are a "west-running brook" with the aim of throwing assumptions back on themselves in order to find "beginning." But, we need to remind the reader, whether eastward or westward, all brooks arrive at the same ocean—which is Christ. Don't mistake us for contrarians. We're not being contrary for the sake of being contrary. We're not set up against everything that is traditional; we're merely trying to distinguish between tradition and truth.

As you read, if you are not familiar with our podcast there's a chance this experience will be like hearing a constant punch line without knowing the joke. This can be awkward. There's a lot of background, context, vocabulary and shared experience in these pages. (It might serve you well to listen to our recommended podcasts on our website. *theocast.org*) But, if this sense of an "inside joke" is off-putting please accept our apology. This was not our intention. There's a fair amount of winsomeness in the pages that follow. This comes from a genuine place. Taking the truth seriously without taking ourselves too seriously is a core value for us. There's the potential to think we're making light of serious realities. This tone can be especially distasteful if your long-held convictions are being challenged. So, please keep reading. You'll discover the pages are laced with a depth of conviction and a reverence for the transcendent realities of God and grace. We're not trying to be insulting. We're trying to be disarming. If this backfires, again, we're sorry.

Additionally, if our arguments resonate with you, we're grateful. Welcome to the reformation. But, you will immediately recognize the tension involved—and potential consequences—of moving away from the familiar and popular. You will begin to think that you're alone and that you're crazy. But you are neither alone nor crazy. There are a lot of you out there. More than you think. Furthermore, these doctrines we're espousing were first espoused by the likes of Calvin and Luther—not to mention a thousand other old-sounding theologians you've not heard of yet! So, these thoughts are not novel. They're our original baseline. Generally, the further back you go toward the beginning of who we are (the Protestant Reformation) the more central the doctrine of assurance is. It is the gravitational force that holds the reformed universe together. Without it, things inevitably drift towards rationalism and the will of man. A stress on the doctrine of assurance sounds odd to us because we are so far removed from the center. Herein, we refer to ourselves as "confessional." It's intended as a contrast to popular evangelicalism. The descriptor is also strategic. By referencing those historic documents— originally set against medieval moralism—which lay out and defend the true Gospel of Christ, we intend to support our arguments with our "founding documents" rather than all the theological amendments which have taken place along the way and shaped our thinking at present. As we argue, we lean upon these confessions as our chief resource. This way you do not have to take our word for it. You can read it for yourself.

Lastly, our prayer is that this brief volume causes you to stop and think about some things you've assumed. The intention is not that you abandon the faith, become anti-traditionalist, or fall into some "cage stage" of anger towards the norm (the "ex-smoker syndrome" as it's called.) Our intention is that Christ becomes clearer and as Calvin once wrote, we may be able to "look straight towards him" having unburied him from years of clutter.

Post Tenebras Lux,

The Boys
Nashville, Tennessee
2018

CHAPTER ONE

You're Not Crazy

The very first thing you do when you sit down to write a book, especially a non-fiction work like this one, is identify your audience. No one writes anything worth reading who is not first writing it to someone who needs to hear it. That's how readers and writers work. Writers find ideas and then readers find writers. You're not looking for a group of people. You are looking for a single person. This individual may be a sample of a larger group, but as far as your writing goes there is only one person. The idea is basic. If you can reach and move this one person with your message, then you can reach and move the rest of them. Therefore, as you write, you are always writing to this single soul out there. Those who write well write small. So, you locate the one individual on the planet who most needs what you have to say. You capture that person in your mind. You see their face. You know their background, interests, experiences and hardships. You know exactly where they are in life because you are writing to them from just beyond the same experience. You know, if given the chance to speak to them, you could put words to their thoughts and feelings. Once you've met, the two of you are bound together by the urgency, content, and importance of your message. Once this happens writing is more of a service and less of a task. Chapters become individual letters written to a friend somewhere on the other side of your heart.

Which brings us to the obvious question. To whom we are writing? Who out there needs to hear what we have to say? Who's the "one person" in our case? It's the person who can't quite put their finger on the problem with their Christian experience. The person who has been told he is free but still feels imprisoned. The person who's been promised she has inherited everything, but feels as if she needs to earn everything. The person who by the blunt-force trauma of life, or having been burned by the Church, or a personal collapse, or the simple wear and tear of the human condition has had his assumptions ripped from his hands. A person wrestling with questions about practices and beliefs that are largely axiomatic in the evangelical sphere. A person timidly peeking out from behind the subculture of Christianity for the very first time. A person who has come to realize that many of the long-held conventions of her faith really aren't hers. A person who thinks he's crazy. A person who assumes she's alone in her skepticism. That's the one person. Our message to him or her is pretty straightforward. You are not crazy, and you are definitely not alone. There is one of you, but there are also many.

We are certain you're not alone. We know this to be a fact. There are myriads of you in the echo chamber of modern evangelicalism asking the same questions at the exact same time. All of you are having trouble putting your finger on the source of your soul's anxiety. Collectively, you are a convergence of skeptics set in motion by events that have been afoot for some time now. You (and we) were inevitable. What you're feeling is the discomfort of cognitive dissonance. Things are no longer lining up. You are fighting to maintain two views of the Christian life that are inevitably contradictory. One is now eclipsing the other.

This sort of thing has happened before. The disenfranchised always seem to find each other in the middle of their confusion. As time passes and eras shift, so does the thinking of those on the thresholds of those eras. The transfer usually takes decades to occur. History itself can be traced by the enormous adjustments in large-scale awareness. The Christian apologist Francis Schaeffer referred to this philosophical changing of the guard as the "line of despair." That line by which the progress of philosophical adjustments can be traced from one age to another.

There are numerous descriptions around regarding the present shift within the evangelical church. It *is* an actual thing. Some refer to it as the post-evangelical era. Evangelicalism, which has dominated the landscape of the Church since the eighteenth century, is now in its twilight. Those forces that caused evangelicalism are now diminished. We would use "post-evangelical" ourselves, excepting that it carries significant theological baggage. Those who originally coined it were part of a new breed of theological liberals. They ended up denying the very heart of Christianity itself and, not surprisingly, faded from relevance. Others would widen their diagnosis. They identify all this as the post-Christian era. That is to say, it is not simply modern evangelicalism, but the whole of Christianity that is on the downturn. Western Christianity is no longer the dominating, or even the accepted worldview. The era of Christianity's influence is now over. We are on the threshold of a post-Christian world. There's a little bit of truth in these explanations. But, the best and most perceptive description we've heard is "pre-Christian." The culture has become so secularized, the Church now faces the same godless and pagan contexts it did when Christ first sent it out into the world. We've circled all the way back around to paganism. Some would say we are on the precipice of a new Dark Age. Obviously, there are traces of hysteria in this view. I expect any day now that the Christian-fiction industry will capitalize on the supply side of this moment. We would suggest clearer heads should prevail. Our preference for this perspective lies in the fact that it offers a hopeful rather than despairing view of the future. It is a moment of real Gospel opportunity. Light shines brightest in the dark.

I don't think it's necessary for the average person to recognize these sorts of meta-categories, or keep up with the musings of ivory-tower philosophers to realize something has changed in the American church. The moment is well documented. Exactly what has happened depends completely on who is being asked, but, the adjustment has been simultaneously felt by all. We've got our hands on different parts of the same elephant at this point, but it's the same beast.

It takes very little effort to point out the distance between where we started and where we've ended up. Evangelical Christianity has morphed into something barely classifiable as biblically Christian. If the early and the modern versions are held up to one another there is barely a resemblance (save the constant reference to Jesus). Their purposes for the atonement are very different from one another. This is not to say our version is anti-Christian. It's more to say it's simply non-Christian. While there is enough Christian residue to move the needle, there isn't really enough to redeem. This drift, in our opinion, is what people feel but can't describe. It's hard to point something out when you are in the middle of it. But, when it's pointed out it becomes annoyingly obvious.

Usually, these sorts of broad observations or pronouncements make conservative evangelicals nervous. They assume it signals a move away from orthodoxy. They sound like buzzwords for progressives. We get this. So, before you roll the eyes of your traditional heart at us, let us add some important footnotes.

We have no intention of throwing the baby out with the

bathwater. We have no desire to scoff "archaic" doctrines and "out of step" theological categories. Perhaps you're expecting that we're about to reject our forefathers, or explain how we've figured it out when others couldn't. In this you'd be wrong. This is not that message. Fact is, we're not offering anything new at all. There is virtually nothing original in the pages that follow. It's quite the opposite. Everything we have to offer can be categorized as "classic." And, our intention is not to reject what came before. Quite to the contrary—we hope to cast off the influence of those who lost touch with it and turned Christianity into an exhausting catalogue of self-improvement techniques. We are especially not interested in offering anything innovative. We bemoan the trends which roll through evangelicalism every decade or so—the same basic set of ideas repackaged for a new generation of spiritual consumer. So, this will not end up being a call to some sort of radicalized Christianity, some new key to spirituality, a special insight into Christian living, spiritual minimalism, or a call to reject traditional structures. For those who keep reading, the outcome is very predictable. You will find yourself standing flat-footed on the ground just outside of the virtual ride known as evangelical Christianity.

It might surprise you to know that we are Calvinists. (We lost some of you right there, didn't we?) Why is this fact relevant? Well, because the stereotype associated with Calvinism proves the above point. Calvinists are not known for being enterprising or novel. After all, if God is sovereign, why be creative? Traditionally speaking, we are the wallflowers at the evangelical dance, the odd ones against the wall. Furthermore, we are reformed in practice. Think "theological unicorns." Basically, we place ourselves in a long-standing and well-defined tradition of doctrine, practice, and piety. We find our home within confessional boundaries set by a multitude of dead theologians. To be fair, many of our Reformed friends would describe us as inconsistently reformed. And, technically, they would be correct. There are aspects of our theology and practice that do not sync up exactly with the Reformed tradition. They hope to persuade us, but we remain theological Bedouins setting up camp in their territory.

The reason for this categorization is simple: Our theological journey has been away from innovation and not toward it. Away from the novel and not toward it. Away from the new and not toward it. Away from the progressive and not toward it. In our expedition for clarity we wandered right out into the *old*. Our coordinates are probably in an opposite location than you would guess. We are way out here on the edges of the modern church geeking out over things most consider irrelevant to daily life, or of which they have never heard. We are not progressive at all. If anything, we're more conventional than before. Theologically speaking, we are 8-track tapes in a digital world. Of course, by our own estimation, we don't see ourselves out on the margin at all. We would say we are closer to the center of what the Christian life was intended to be. Our intention is to demonstrate how far we've all drifted from the original simplicity of faith in Christ.

We maintain, as often as we can, that Christianity never was meant to be so convoluted.

"Deconstructing evangelicalism one bad idea at a time." We regularly use this line in the opener of our podcast. Part of what we do as a ministry is poke at the assumptions within our collective experience as evangelicals. This is exactly how we end up saying things people have been thinking, and asking questions they have been too afraid to ask. It's part of our appeal. We're not the first to attempt a systematic deconstruction of American Christianity in an effort to get to something more pure and consistent. If you are reading this book you've most likely been engaged in it yourself. It needs to be noted that deconstruction does not always end well. Many who start to pull back the layers are so discouraged at what they find, they end up leaving the faith all together. There are some notable examples. Bart Ehrman, once a rising star in the field of textual criticism, started questioning some assumptions and eventually left the faith altogether. He not only left, but also stands quite outside it as an apologist committed to discrediting Christianity at every opportunity. He has written a number of books arguing against Christian theism. One of his more popular books, *God's Problem*, suggests the problem of evil eliminates the existence of God altogether.

Then there's Rob Bell, the best-selling author and cutting-edge evangelical pastor. He too started challenging the norms, only to gradually vacate classic Christianity. He now stands outside of our boundary lines somewhere between theism and mysticism. Like Erhman, Bell is also taking runs at the Church and its traditional structures. His farewell to orthodoxy was *Love Wins* where he espoused universalism. The point is, deconstruction can be dangerous if one does not keep his head in the process.

Our aim in dismantling many of the strange components within evangelicalism is not to push people away from Christianity, but nearer to it. We are aware that many of the observations we make can be disturbing to the mainline mindset, but we also know that a little disruption can lead to greater clarity. Take for example our observation that the modern concept of "spiritual disciplines" is mainly an adaptation of medieval mysticism. This one takes a minute to sink in. Immediately, when people hear this they assume we mean people no longer need to read their Bibles, or pray, or be disciplined. But that is not what we mean. What we mean is this approach to the Christian life is a late development in evangelicalism. It is a codified spirituality influenced by pietism and mysticism. Prior to its development, Christians prayed and read their Bibles and disciplined themselves for godliness—only their motivation was not increased levels of spirituality, but access to Christ in the establishment of their faith. In other words, there is another way to approach the Christian life that employs the same means but for very different reasons. But you would never know this if we did not point it out. In fact, we would not know this if someone had not pointed it out to us. In this way we are not tearing essential things down, but getting down to essential things.

We know people are frustrated by the pressures placed on them by current evangelical theology and practice including both the popular and fundamentalist versions. Our intent at pulling on these threads is not so they would leave the faith, but that they would rediscover it.

Rather constantly we receive communications from people wandering in the wilderness of this present moment; every one of them unaware they are thinking the same thing countless others are thinking. All of them write the same message, completely unaware others have taken up the pen to express the same sentiments. *"How did Christianity ever become so complicated? Where has this simplicity of faith been my whole life? You guys are really on to something here. Thank you."* Among the joys of our ministry, we count two as primary. One is connecting the ever-expanding network of like-minded pilgrims. The other is informing them that "our message" is not our message at all. It's the one that predates the present confusion and was the predominant perspective for the majority of the Church's history. Actually, *we* aren't on to anything. The thanks belongs to those who saw it first. It's really been here the whole time beneath our lives gathering dust in the church. Like how Saint Augustine's writings gathered dust in a monastery until an Augustinian monk, frustrated by the despair of the monastic lifestyle, fell upon freedom by reading the primary sources of Augustine for himself. The monk became a contradiction of the very institution to which he belonged. It happens this way for reformers.

Underneath all of this complexity we have come to confuse with Christianity, there exists a simplicity that actually sustains the weary pilgrim. And that is our fundamental message. There is a sustainable Christianity available to the child of God. There is a hope that lies quite outside of you. There is a piety derived from something besides fear. There is a repentance that leads to liberation. There is a motivation of obedience emanating from the impulse of love. There is an assurance that finds its ground in realities bigger than you. Some of you feel this right now, but don't know where to go. This is for you. There is a way out of this clutter. Or, to be more precise, a way back into the simple.

We are also aware of another audience—the collateral one. Those who don't have the same level of concern, or angst, but are curious nonetheless. We write with you in mind as well. But, in order for this to work we need you to do something for us. Otherwise, you won't make the journey. We need you to suspend your accumulative Christian experience for awhile, like when you subconsciously suspend disbelief allowing for the coincidences that hold movie plots together. If you don't let those things go (temporarily) you will never hear us. You certainly won't be able to enjoy the story. So, we need you to suspend your assumptions for a moment and accept the basic plotline. We realize it's hard to un-think things you've always assumed. All our evangelical habits are rather ingrained by now. There are instincts you've developed over decades of practice. They're involuntary at this point. You always reach up with the same dominant hand. We're asking you to reach up with the opposite. This exercise will be a little like throwing left-handed. It will be a little awkward. You will be a little self-conscious. Things will seem out of place. Like driving in the UK. Same vehicle, same steering wheel, same pedals, same dashboard and same windshield, but in very opposite places of where they are normally located. It takes a minute to figure this out. But it will come to you. Let's start at the beginning.

You Are Now Leaving Pietism

We think most evangelical narratives trend something like this. When you were a child, under the guidance of your Sunday school teacher, you asked Jesus into your heart. You've been in the church your entire life. Or, while attending a summer camp as a student you committed your life to Christ. You spent a lot of time journaling in your younger years. Or, after having "backslid" for most of college, you finally came back to the church and "rededicated" your life to God. Shockingly, at the very moment you graduated, you got your life together. It's uncanny timing. Possibly, your experience includes some combination of the above. Or, maybe your experience includes all of these. This is not uncommon. Regardless, at whatever stage it all became real for you and you identified publicly as a Christian, we can predict what happened next. The church immediately began explaining *what Christians do*. You started attending a class on what you should be doing now that you are a Christian. Or someone handed you a book explaining the basic disciplines and practices of the

Christian life: *How to start a daily Bible reading plan. How to have "devotions." How to develop a habit of prayer. How to join a church. How to attend a church. How to get plugged into a church. How to give to a church. How to be sanctified. How to become godly. How to avoid sin. How to curb sinful patterns. How to worship. How to evangelize. How to have a testimony.* You know exactly what we're talking about. It's all the stuff Christians do that make Christians Christian.

We can also predict what didn't take place at the very same moment. At no time then (and possibly since), did anyone explain *what* happened to you. No one took the time to explain *who you are* now that you are in Christ. No one described the cosmic wonder of what being *in Christ* actually means. The Church pointed you inward to what you should be doing, but they never pointed you outward to what was done for you. It was a message of *in*. It was not a message of *out*. The Church saddled you with duty, but neglected to explain your identity. For you, Christianity is about an improved morality, or an increased happiness, but it is most certainly not about *being*. There was no schematic on who you are now as compared to before.. You are forgiven by God. You are just before God. You are adopted in Christ. You are a child of God. You are freed from the condemnation which once hung over you. This is the fundamental glitch within the evangelicalism system. We would argue that life for the believer is fueled by a constant flow of good news. *"God is good with you child"* is our ultimate confidence as pilgrims. To put it simply: The

Christian life is intended to be lived from "status forward." Living it the other way around is fraught with frustration and fear. If our lives are spent striving to keep our standing intact, there is only despair. It's like leaping back over the wall of the very prison from which we were liberated. If, on the other hand, we are living from our standing outward, their freedom is as far as the heart can see.

We are redeemed in the exact same order we fell: *from status to life*. In the act of faith our status is restored and then our lives are transformed. This is the classic distinction between justification (position) and sanctification (transformation) essential to our confession as Protestants. You are set free and then you are being set free. *Who we are* is recovered and then *how we live* follows. Redemption never flows in the opposite direction. The streams never cross. In Adam, the very first thing to go for mankind was our position. In Christ, the very first thing to be restored is our position.

Guilt is such a normative experience for us we can't comprehend life without it. We have no way of knowing the shock Adam felt as it entered his heart for the first time. All we know is what he did. In shame and confusion he hid himself. The one (shame) stemmed from the other (guilt). No longer was man safe in the presence of his Creator. Dread, once foreign to his existence, was now his habitation. No longer did he rest in a state of innocence. As the corruption of his human frame took hold, a virus was downloaded into his DNA and transferred to all of his posterity. Therefore, every human is born bearing all three of these burdens: guilt, shame, and corruption. It is the order of our fallen existence. We are hemmed in by the same sense of dread that Adam experienced. Shame is the baseline of our existence. We are born hiding.

Salvation is a reversal of these effects. Our redemption follows the same sequence as our condemnation. The very first thing that is restored is the very first thing that was lost: Our standing before God—justification). Our guilt is removed. Our shame is covered. Our condemnation is satisfied. All of this takes place in and by the person of Christ. This is the classic language of substitution. In a moment our status as sinners is irrevocably reversed. There is no longer a reason to cower, or to flee the presence of God. "In Christ" we are invited to come out of hiding. For those who've exhausted themselves running from certain judgment, peace is the hardest reality to accept. It is not natural to us. This "body of death" we carry with us sustains the impulse to flee. A fear lingers. And, yet, there is no need to fear. He is the judge. He is our Father. This co-existence of such contradictory realities (acceptance and rejection) creates an enormous tension in the believer.

In the sweetest bit of irony it's actually the grace of God that sets off this cataclysmic disturbance in our lives. Disapproval is normal. Approval is not. We are actually deserving of judgment, but because of God's grace we're also righteous. A lingering sense of guilt still echoes in our persons and can overwhelm our hearts. Because sin is still a struggle for us we constantly expect to be condemned, but we will not be condemned. We are not condemnable although everything in us tells us we are. This contradiction of experience is normal for the Christian and exactly why Paul declared, "There is no condemnation." In this statement he was not merely being dramatic for effect. He was not merely ending his argument for justification. He was reading our minds. He was answering the question that nags at our souls. "Is it true?" Paul declares, "It is true brothers and sisters. Now go live in it."

The Apostle Paul describes redemption as a sort of cosmic prison break. On the largest scale we were set free from our previous identity as enemies. We were set free from the bondage of sin, condemnation of the Law and threat of eternal judgment. By grace through faith in Christ our status is transferred from enemy to beloved. We live everyday in the rhythm of this truth. The redemption of our humanity (which is ongoing) flows naturally from the recovery of our positions (which was instant). But, we are typically handed a view of the Christian life that runs off in the opposite direction. Peace and security is a carrot dangling from a necessity "to get better." What we get is the real sense that we should run for our lives, when actually we have nothing to fear. Our burden is to become the type of people God would accept and remain that way. As we've come to understand, doing leads to being. It's all backwards. The real Christian message is the opposite. Being leads to living.

If Christianity addresses any issue, it is that we can never reach a level of perfection in which God would be inclined to accept us. We are imperfect. We are an infinite distance from ever reaching it. This sense of imperfection sits on our souls like a weight. We must be perfect to be accepted by God, but aren't and never can be. Enter the Gospel. God—motivated by His unconditional love—met the requirement of perfection in His Son for us. Therefore, we are freed from the necessity to be perfect people by the perfection of another. Perfection is no longer a condition for which we strive. It is a gift we receive. God met the standards of His own righteousness so it would no longer hang over our heads. This is the very sphere in which we live and breathe. As Steinbeck so insightfully wrote in *East of Eden*: "And now that you don't have to be perfect, you can be good." Now that we no longer worry about the condition of perfection, all that is left is to live.

As he instructed the newborn church, the Apostle Paul began with *who* and not *how*. One inevitably follows the other, but they are never reversed. Paul himself was delivered from a religion that had the sequence backwards. Therefore, his Gospel moved from identity to life. Ultimately, what sets us free is not what we do for God, but what's been done by God for us. As Paul describes it, we have been delivered from a tyrant and are presently running free under the rule and reign of a benevolent Lord. We are citizens of a different city journeying in the land of the in-between. Having a burden lifted, but still burdened. You are free, but not quite home free.

The apostle's mind-boggling riff in Romans chapter six is not a description of the interior of the Christian life as it is normally described. He's not in the weeds of *how*. He's up in the air of *what*. The reason you should not do certain things any longer is because you don't' have to do those things any longer. That is not who you are any longer. You are now free. This is the basic meaning of freedom in the Christian sense. We have been set free from who we were. We are freed to live under the righteousness of Christ. You have been transferred from one domain to another. Your status has been moved from slave to child.

Not until very deep into the Christian life do most of us discover the liberating effects of our identity. Most live in ignorance for a long time. All these years later, hustling for some sense of assurance, we come to discover we're the heirs of an infinite fortune. It's been at our disposal all along. Until this awareness descends on us, the Christian life will always be more or less approached as an ongoing transaction with God: To the degree we are performing our duties, we are accepted. God is like the disapproving dad who implicitly communicates to his child, "I will love you when you please me." We spend the majority of our Christian lives struggling to earn something we freely possess.

This whole ironic progression reminds me of those home-remodel shows where someone buys an older home looking for the purpose of flipping it. As they assess damage their attention inevitably turns to the floor. In a corner of a room they grab a handful of carpet and begin pulling. They're always looking for the same thing. And occasionally they find it. Right under their feet, buried under layers of time, is a beautiful hardwood floor. At some point in the past, covering the natural with the synthetic seemed like a good idea. In a moment—once exhumed and restored—the entire room is pulled together. All the accents are drawn out. The space begins to make sense. Coming to see our Christian life in light of our position in Christ is like that. Once it's uncovered, everything else comes together and makes sense. Things are put in order. It can stay hidden buried under layers of stuff for a very long time. The question is: Why don't we sit our friends down at the beginning of this pilgrimage and put it out there? *You need to sit down for this. There's something I have to tell you. I've got good news and I've got good news. Which do you want first?* Where has this been? The treasures of the child of God are some of the worst-kept secrets in the Bible.

This perspective does not make much sense to people when you first start talking about it. *Who you are* seems more like a ticker running across the bottom of the Christian life. It's an afterthought in the rearview of redemption. Position does not seem very practical to us. How you're progressing seems more urgent. Done is past. Do is present. This is a fundamental misunderstanding. Identity may not be the only thing, but there is nothing else without it.

For the longest time I have carried my passport with me everywhere I go. I don't remember why exactly, but it remains in a pocket of my computer bag. I suppose if it's always with you, you never have to wonder where it is. As far as ID goes it's total overkill. There's not a single time I have used it while in my home country. After all, who needs a passport at home? A passport is for travel abroad. It grants individuals the rights and privileges of their U.S. citizenship while on foreign soil. Usually, that laminated little blue booklet means very little to us. The rights and privileges it grants are merely words on a page. However, the moment you leave your native soil, your passport and its proof of identity is the most important item you possess. The more foreign things are the more valuable it becomes. When the plane begins to descend into Beirut, Lebanon, the fine print on who you are is the most important thing you have.

In a manner of speaking, we are a long way from home. This is exactly why our position in Christ is immediately central and inevitably practical. The Gospel needs to play on a loop in our hearts. Because we journey through the fallout zone of our rebellion still carrying the burden on our fallen flesh, sin assails our life from every angle. This includes the interior one. The Law of God overwhelms our conscience as we are constantly tripping the alarm of doubt. Guilt and shame arise like bad memories of the soul. This far out from home, the fine print of the Gospel is the only reality that will calm our hearts. Despite how we may feel while here in "the valley of the shadow of death" we are confident He will bring us home. Since our status in Christ is most often the first thing we doubt, it is the main thing to remember.

OK. Let's stop here for a moment. We need to get something out of the way. There are some who object to the above line of reasoning along very predictable lines. Two central ones come to mind. One objection concerns God. Some would say placing too great an emphasis on God's favor towards us diminishes His other attributes. All this talk of "Abba Father" has a tendency to eclipse the more threatening elements of God's nature. God is Holy. God is Righteous. God is Judge. God is to be feared. God is to be reverenced. God is to be approached with trepidation. The implicit accusation is that we are minimizing God's transcendence in order for people to feel better about themselves. What is our response? This is completely backward from our point. We draw attention to God's favor *because* people despair of who they are. And because there is nothing they can do about it. This is precisely why proclaiming the good news to a Christian is as valid as proclaiming it to a non-Christian. They must be reassured that what God has promised is true despite the fact the opposite seems real. It is exactly because God is Holy and we are not that the Gospel is proclaimed.

The other objection concerns the Christian. Some would argue that focusing so heavily upon these objective realities (justification, adoption) eliminates any sense of the subjective ones. If you tell people they are safe no matter what, they will take you up on it. As the logic goes, an overemphasis on grace erodes any sense of duty in sanctification and the fight against sin. No one is sanctified by simply sitting around and thinking about their identity in Christ. We are obligated to fight against sin every day. Again, we would argue that this is the very misunderstanding we are pointing out. In reality, grace is the reason our conflict with sin exists. Had the Spirit never given us life we never would have the impulse to fight against death. The struggle against sin is an inevitable reality for all those in Christ. This much is assumed in Scripture. What we are arguing becomes very clear at this point. It is exactly because the Christian is at war with sin (both within and without) that our identity in Christ must constantly be brought to the foreground. It's not a question of *if* we will battle. It's actually not even a question. Were it not for a barrage of good news, the weary pilgrim would despair. The fine print of who we are in Christ is the basis of our resistance to who we were.

This is the tension that lies at the heart of Protestantism. It is the very riddle of the universe that sent a monk into despair. And, it was his eventual solution to the riddle that caused the Reformation. As we journey, we are both. "Saint and sinner at the same time!" We deserve hell, but are children nonetheless. He is our Judge, but He is also our Father. We are condemnable, but will never be condemned. We are unworthy of His presence, but are invited into it. If it were *either/or*, rather than *both/and*, there would be no Gospel. As one theologian put it, "A man may be righteous and yet be unholy. Were this not so there could be no salvation for sinners." This paradox in our experience is precisely why we live in earshot of the Gospel. Our efforts—even as Christians—will never rise to the level of God's acceptance. And the pain of our insufficiency is constantly with us. How is it a Holy God calls a sinner like me child? How can He be just and yet my justifier at the same time? The reminder of who we are fits perfectly in this little compartment of misery.

Not a day has passed in my children's lives that I have not leaned into their souls in one way or another and reminded them how much I love them. I have considered it among my greatest responsibilities as a dad. Our home is a constant outpouring of affection. *I love you. I am proud of you. You are so gifted.* I have learned from the absence of such affirmation in my own childhood how invaluable it is to the human heart. Even now as they are launching into adulthood, I am running beside their lives shouting encouragement. This has been one of the most sublime joys of my life. Why have I done this? Mainly because it's true. But, also because they need it imprinted on their souls. As they move forward in life and everything around them changes, they will remember the one thing that remains the same: They are accepted.

There are two types of people in the world. Everyone lines up in one of two rows. The groups can be identified by various assessments. There are those who upon hearing of a chance of rain take an umbrella with them. And, there are those who don't. There are those who merge early when a lane of traffic is coming to an end. And, there are late mergers. And then, spiritually speaking, there are those who constantly look back at their progress as a way of assuring themselves that God is good with them. Those in this group can never quite catch their breath. They have to keep moving. There's too much ground to make up between who they *are* and who they *should* be. They measure their life in increments of *should* and *am*. And then there are those who don't spend too much time looking back. When they do, all they see is how greatly they underestimated their corruption from the start. They mainly look up and take in the perpetual sunrise of redemption breaking overhead. They breathe in deep breaths of Gospel air and rest their souls under its constant declaration: "It is finished." While they do progress, they don't really keep tabs on it. They are too distracted by the scenery of grace. They measure their life in increments of *finished* and *am*.

Since status comes first, the chief and most ferocious battle of our lives is not what we should do or shouldn't do. It's *who* we are that we fight to believe. This world in every way is set against the reality of God's goodness towards us. It's so hard to believe given who we really are. This is undeniable in our Christian experience. As pilgrims traveling this shattered existence, what hounds us the whole way is doubt. We are struggling not to behave, but to believe. This is the central difference between a Christianity which points inward to the Christian (pietism) and one which is pointing outward (confessional) to Christ. Even though our status has been restored our corruption still remains. The beacon of our guilt still goes off in the rubble of our fallen natures. Although we are reminded we are children of God there are countless times we feel more like His enemy. The fear of "how can he love me?" is always encroaching upon the truth of "while we were yet enemies." As we journey there is a real and demonstrative struggle with guilt, shame, and doubt. They feed off each other. It is hard to believe that we are beloved when we feel condemned. The battle is believing—against all odds—that what God has declared about us is actually true in light of what we know of ourselves. The actual battle of the Christian life is the one of faith. Not faithfulness from us, but faith in Him—believing that what He has declared us to be in His son is true, when what we are on the ground seems very different.

Coming to Terms with Nothing to Do

Americans are busy people. Life in our world is one unending and frenzied task list. All our domestic chaos is compounded by the perpetual distraction of technology. Those advances intended to create efficiency only create more to do and less time in which to do it. Our immediate access to everything leaves us with nothing of meaning in return. There's little gravity or rhythm in our existence. I don't think we're totally aware of the effect all of this has on our persons. But, if you sit still for any amount of time, you'll notice the side effects of frenetic. It's like that ringing in your ear that becomes obvious the moment you enter into silence. Similarly, if we are ever alone with our thoughts we can hear a ringing in our souls. I feel the tension whenever I'm on vacation with my family. I usually take two weeks at a time. It's hard for me to let go. For the first couple of days I'm still tied to my devices, not really gone from where I was before. My mind is still fully engaged in all those "things to do." Catching glances of disapproval from my wife and kids, when I finally sit in that chair on the beach, my family flanking me on all sides like an intervention, the buzzing starts. I can't sit there. I have to get up and do something. (Once on a cruise I walked about fifteen miles around the deck of the ship on the first day.) After about seven days I relax and am finally content merely sitting there.

My problem is simple. I have no idea what to do with nothing to do. It's hard to get comfortable in that space where there are no expectations and where personal value is not tied to performance and accomplishment. That's an awkward space for me to fit my life. But, when I finally unclench my mind from all those distractions, I come back to myself and the things that matter. I'm comfortable in my own thoughts. But, doing nothing is hard. Evangelical Christians suffer from the same malady. Our faith is about doing, more than it is about being. We have no idea what to do with nothing to do. The idea of simply resting in God's approval in Christ, without getting up and doing something, is foreign to us. I'd argue that the idea of doing nothing is offensive to us—a waste of time and opportunity. Our Christianity is like a free-market system where hard work and ingenuity is rewarded greater approval ratings. I think we all feel this way. This is one of the reasons we answer that ubiquitous question, "How's your faith?" in the negative. "It could be better." Or, "I'm not praying as much as I should." Why do we answer this way? Because that's how we measure success in our Christian experience. What would we think about a different answer? "There's not been a lot of activity lately, mainly, I've been trusting in God's good favor for me. I'm striving more to rest than I am striving to improve." To most evangelical Christians this sounds like compromise, failure, and negligence. But, biblically speaking, it's the sweet spot of our faith. Resting is harder than doing. Furthermore, the real challenge is resting while striving. Striving for striving's sake comes naturally to us. Resting does not.

"For if Joshua had given them rest, God would not have spoken of another day later on. So then, there remains a Sabbath rest for the people of God, for whoever has entered God's rest has also rested from his works as God did from his." (Hebrews 4:8-10)

As you look on all these eons later, it is apparent that the land of Canaan was analogous to the real and greater Promised Land. That patch of land is described as a place of rest for a people who had known only struggle and wandering. The promise of rest was always on the horizon. Rest is where their faith was leading them. But Canaan was merely a shadow, and Jesus was the substance that cast the shadow by the light of history. Jesus is the Sabbath rest to which both the Sabbath and the Promised Land pointed. Everything points to Jesus. Jesus is the object by which we cease striving from that greater struggle which assails our existence. In Jesus, even as we struggle forward, we are able to rest by faith. By faith we have been ushered into the rest to which all those shadows pointed. At the highest level, all of sinful humanity is perpetually pushed along by a sense of our unworthiness before

God. Life is comprised of struggle and wandering. There is no hope on the horizon. Israel's burden pointed to the universal one, the weight every human being experiences inherently. Enter Jesus. He is our rest. In Him alone can we "cease our striving." Metaphorically speaking, as it concerns our condition before God, we can finally rest. He is our stopping point.

This book is intended to help the reader find this rare space of rest in Christ. By this we do not mean inactivity. We mean that place where striving and rest meet. When this broken world does all the damage it can, when our sinful hearts are tormented by our consciences, when our exhausted spirits doubt the favor of God, when we daily fight to the death against our flesh, and when all the other broken people on this planet wound us, there remains one place where there is nothing left to do. There is a place of rest: A quiet little spot on our journey where we can finally sit there and come to terms with nothing to do. This is *A Pilgrim's Guide to Rest*.

CHAPTER TWO

Leaving Pietism

I n his *Institutes of the Christian Religion,* John Calvin, the great
reformer, takes up a discussion concerning something he
identifies as "implicit faith." At this point the writer is deep
into his debate with the Catholic Church. What's notable is that
"implicit faith" *(fides implicita)* comes up in his monumental section
on the doctrine of faith. What's also notable about this topic is the
peculiar indignation it receives from Calvin. It's a hot button for
him. I'm not even kidding. Here's Calvin in his own words:

> *This evil, then, like innumerable others, must be
> attributed to the Schoolmen (i.e. philosophical
> theologians) who have, as it were, drawn a veil over
> Christ to hide him. Unless we look straight toward
> him, we shall wander through endless labyrinths. But*

besides wearing down the whole force of faith and almost annihilating it by their obscure definition, they have fabricated the fiction of "implicit faith." Bedecking the grossest ignorance with this term, they ruinously delude poor, miserable folk. Furthermore, to state truly and frankly the real fact of the matter, this fiction not only buries but utterly destroys true faith. Is this what believing means – to understand nothing, provide only that you submit your feeling obediently to the church?

Sounds like me ranting about my homeowners association; which is, of course, the most necessary evil known to man. So what *is* implicit faith and why is Calvin so agitated? In Calvin's day implicit faith was a reference to the level of trust the common man placed in the teachings of the Church without understanding what the Church was actually teaching. Implicit faith basically means that what people could not grasp explicitly they had to trust implicitly. In simpler terms, it was a blind faith in the Church. People trusted that the teachings of the Church were true, or that traditions were essential, but had no way of verifying it. Due to ignorance, medieval saints were at the submission of the Church concerning spiritual realities. Now technically, Calvin did admit there is a broader sense in which every believer has to trust implicitly that which they cannot grasp explicitly. There are a lot of mysteries surrounding the nature and ways of God. But this is not what the Church meant by "implicit faith." Actually, it was how the Church kept men trapped in darkness. The Church had created what Calvin describes as an endless "labyrinth" of codes, doctrines, traditions, and rituals. People entered the maze of religious realities trusting that it eventually let out into salvation. It never did. It only led people deeper in. Of course, as Calvin points out, the Church actually used the complicated web of traditions and the ignorance of its subjects to protect the Church's authority and its bottom line.

This is why Calvin went after the concept and called it a "pious ignorance." The Church had blinded people to the simplicity of a genuine faith in the person of Christ. Saving faith was an explicit trust in a singular object, not an implicit trust in an institution and its mazes. All those additional steps, principles, measures, and tasks the Church had created over the centuries had buried the Gospel of God's grace under a pile of religious clutter. The only way the common believer could see the truth of the Gospel was to look "straight toward" Christ. They had to ignore all the stuff and look to Jesus alone. That's what happened in the Reformation. Christ was exhumed from the tradition of the Church and placed above all other traditions and doctrines of men, as the sole object of faith for those who would be justified. Calvin concludes this section this way:

> *But let us not tarry longer over refuting them;*
> *we merely admonish the reader to compare these*

doctrines with ours (the reformed faith). The very
clarity of truth will of itself provide a sufficiently
ready refutation.

I love that. "The Gospel will speak for itself." When tradition is held up to the Gospel, all nonessentials fall away.

The reason I bring this up is probably obvious. I've already tipped my hand. While not in exactly the same way, evangelical Christians suffer from something similar to an implicit faith. In a comparable fashion, we trust that the traditions of the evangelical church handed down to us are both true and essential. I don't mean to say that all of our practices are unbiblical ("error"), but, I do mean that much of our content and practice are non-biblical ("traditional") and nonessential ("derived"). It's what we do because it's we've always done. We've got our own repertoire of steps, principles, measures, and tasks, resulting in our own distinct subculture. Much of what we assume to be genuine Christian practice and belief may push us further away from the true Gospel and not toward it. Christ is hidden from view. New laws and obligations are placed where faith in Christ belongs. In Calvin's day *Sola Cristus* (Christ Alone) was the moment people were able to separate tradition from biblical truth. In that moment the complexity of their inherited religion was set aside for the simplicity of faith in Christ.

I see this same process of discovery taking place all around me in the evangelical church. That moment unsuspecting people catch a glimpse of the gospel of grace and the simplicity of true saving faith, and step out of the chaos. It's a startling contrast. I don't mean that people are walking away from the faith. I mean they are walking back toward it as it is recovered for them in the reformed confessional tradition. When Calvin said "our" doctrine would make the truth clear, this is what he meant. Those reformed defenses of the Gospel and rich confessions in history have the same effect today as they did then. They make the error and nonessentials obvious by contrast. Part of our problem in this is that we don't exactly understand how we got where we are and what has shaped our thinking. If we could trace our lineage back, I think we'd be better able to distinguish essential from traditional and immediately exchange complexity for simplicity. Like digging Christ out from under years of our own religious artifacts.

Our Theological Ancestry

Everything comes from something. Not exactly rocket science, I know. Cause and effect is basic physics. Trees come from seeds. Seeds come from trees. This reality is self-evident in our material existence. But the same cause-and-effect event could also be applied to more existential, cultural, and philosophical realities. We don't normally think in a cause-and-effect way as it concerns larger cultural and social realities, but we should. We stand to learn a lot about who we are as people. Take history for instance. History is not a static set of facts. History is a meta-narrative of cause and effect filled with figures, movements, philosophical shifts, wars, politics, and cultures all leading to the development of specific eras. Whatever country or culture we call home came from somewhere and was shaped by an incalculable number of circumstances. When we examine the interconnections of all these particulars, history begins to shed light on the present. Something led to us. These influences are deep in our cultural DNA.

Most people who find history boring do so because they don't see the drama in the details. But you only need to ask one question to pique the interest of the most resistant historian: *What if?* What if gunpowder had never been invented? What if Hitler had never been born? What if the technology for the hydrogen bomb had never been discovered? What if the Twinkie was never created? Change any number of incidents, people, or moments in history (even inconsequential ones) and things turn out very differently. *We* turn out very differently. From this angle it is easy to see how events occurring thousands of years before we were born are essential to who we are. Things come from things.

Religion is no exception. It too is cause and effect. I teach a church-history course at the local church I pastor. My approach is slightly different than normal. I teach history backwards. This is because I want people to see the cause and effect of church history. I start in the present moment and work all the way back to Jesus. Everything in between Jesus and now is connected. To make the connections I practice what is called an "archeology of the present." I dig up the characteristics of the present moment and then ask, "How did we get here?" and "Where did our habits and commitments come from?" Then we go digging around in the past. We move backward through time to figure out who we are in the present. There are certain moments and innumerable forces that gave birth to the movements and religious commitments of modern evangelicals. As the saying goes, you have to climb a tree before you fall out of it. Evangelicalism came from somewhere and was driven out onto the branches of history by specific influences. In the case of evangelicalism, the story of how we arrived at this present moment is one of the more bizarre tales in the history of the church. There's never been anything quite like us. There's little doubt we'd be unrecognizable to our protestant forefathers.

Defining evangelicalism is notoriously difficult. This is because, by definition, it is indefinable and indeterminate. It's a movement more than it is a religion. It's not a denomination either, although it includes about forty thousand of them. If you live in America, call yourself a Christian, and are not Catholic, or Orthodox, etc., you're most likely an evangelical. We're born evangelicals. This includes you and me. We attend evangelical churches. We are committed to the religious ethos of evangelicalism. We have lived in it all our lives. But if asked to define what it means to be an evangelical Christian, most can't. It's like trying to explain water to fish. The definitions offered by preachers, historians, and theologians differ from one another in slight ways. They all use terms like *Bible*, *Jesus*, *evangelism*, and *missions* to clarify who evangelicals are, but these terms could just as well be applied to Christians outside of western evangelicalism. When asked to explain the origins of evangelicalism people draw the same sort of blank. There's no real knowledge of the specific events and the underlying philosophies that led to us. This rootlessness is typical of evangelicalism. For most, it simply is Christianity.

Here's my own definition of evangelicalism: It's what happens when Christian and American are mixed together. More simply it is "Americanity." A uniquely American way to be a Christian, determined by the socio-political forces within and around American culture and history. The moment the Christian faith landed in the New World, the result was this peculiar Americanized mixture of Christianity. It could be argued that evangelicalism was inevitable.

Think of it this way; there is no such thing as a "Christian American." Obviously, there are Americans who are Christians (and Christians who are Americans). But, there is no such thing as a "Christian American." Here's a logical equivalency. Many evangelicals believe there is such a thing as a Christian plumber. We look for the fish on their vans and hire them because they are Christian plumbers. It's our duty as Christians. But, there is no such thing as a Christian plumber. There is no biblical way to unclog a toilet. There *are* Christians who *are* plumbers by trade. And they unclog toilets like every non-Christian plumber does. But there are no Christian plumbers. The underlying belief system that creates the idea of a Christian plumber is a product of the over-spiritualized subculture of evangelicalism. The concept of the Christian plumber is actually bad for Christianity *and* plumbing since the combination dilutes the meaning of each. The religious concoction is a part of our confusion. This is what I mean when I say there is no such thing as a "Christian American." There are Americans who are Christians and Christians who are Americans, but, there are no Christian Americans. Our odd mixture of American and Christian is what it means to be an evangelical. This sense is deeply embedded in our world. This is the tree from which we fell.

One-Third American

Where did we come from? If you mailed our evangelical DNA off to Ancestry.com our pie chart would come back primarily in thirds divided by three major heritages. First, as mentioned above, we are part *American*. This trait lies behind many of our primary religious instincts. For example, this is where our heavily individualized faith comes from. We are fiercely independent as Americans. Religious freedom is an inalienable right and seeps out into our practice as Christians. It manifests itself in our resistance to any authoritative doctrinal standard. No church or individual can tell us what to believe. As individuals we are free to choose where and how to worship. This has led to all the religious variety in our context—otherwise known as denominationalism. Our evangelical family portrait includes fundamentalists on one side, extreme charismatics on the other, and everything else in-between.

Furthermore, the unlimited option of religious styles available to the individual has resulted in an ecclesiastical free market where churches compete for congregants like brands competing for your business. Evangelicals are very much consumers. So, you might also say evangelicalism is what happens when consumerism and Christianity are joined together. Ultimately, we are free to think and decide for ourselves. Excluding the Bible, there is no unifying standard of belief. But all our disagreements regarding what the Bible actually teaches has led to mass doctrinal confusion. No one is in charge. Outside explicit heresy, no one can censure any other person or group of people. It's doctrinal chaos. Evangelicalism is a perpetual theological food fight at the family table. The lack of certainty that this mess creates is one of the reasons that younger generations are migrating to high-church contexts. The certitude is comforting.

One-Third Revivalists

We are also part *revivalists*. When the American religious landscape began to take shape it was heavily influenced by what is known as *revivalism*. Most of us know revivalism by its more common name—the Great Awakenings. These massive spiritual movements of the eighteenth and nineteenth century did more to shape who we are as evangelicals than nearly anything else. Whether you know it or not, most all of your Christian tradition and current practice is derived directly from the awakenings. I realize, for many, criticizing the Great Awakenings, which includes stalwarts such as Jonathan Edwards, is like criticizing a basket of puppies. What heartless sociopath doesn't like puppies? But honestly, not everything that came down to us from the awakenings was a "good." There are numerous unfortunate elements that still impact us to this day. This is especially true of the Second Great Awakening and the influences that trickled down to later generations.

In many ways, revivalism (and its impact on our religious minds) was also an inevitable occurrence in early American religious life. Many of our current defects can be traced directly to this moment. Here's what I mean: As the traditional churches from Europe began to get on their feet in America, they soon realized their significant disadvantage. The liberty of the individual, the inherent suspicion of hierarchy, and the pursuit of personal happiness did not fit neatly within the immobile and hierarchical traditions. Confessions and catechesis were inefficient means to gather Christians, direct their lives, and lead people to Christ. What power and influence churches had in their native land was neutered by the Bill of Rights. As people resisted the religious establishment new strategies were necessary to reach people for Christ. So preachers changed their theology and methods to meet the challenge. As a result, Christianity became very personalized and pragmatic. To gather people, preachers had to relate on individual and immediately practical levels. It was a matter of supply and demand. This is why we inherently gravitate to relevant and practical messaging. We "Christian Americans" love messages that tease out our potential. It's in our DNA.

There is a lot of revivalism's influence lying around modern evangelicalism. It's virtually everywhere. A major effect concerns our understanding of conversion. OK. Let's make a distinction here. The doctrine of conversion and *conversionism* are two altogether different realities. The former is what God does in the heart through regeneration. Conversion is when our regenerated heart is manifest in time and space by our public confession of Christ. God does this supernaturally. The latter is a uniquely American phenomenon. It is a strategy intended to garner "decisions for Jesus." "Decisionalism," as it is known. It's a technique of evangelism aimed at converting sinners by creating a crisis of the soul. If people were not part of established churches preachers had to find other ways to "convert" them. So they got on horses, rode out to the frontier, constructed makeshift churches and started preaching "fire and brimstone" sermons. Their aim was to create a crisis of mind and heart in the listener. Invitations were offered, aisles were cleared, decisions were called for, and wailing benches constructed in order that sinners might be converted to Christ. These little revivals were pervasive. The evangelist rode into town, lit the locals up with messages of damnation, logged their conversion rates, got back on their horses and rode on to the next town.

Imperceptibly, the practices associated with "conversionism" changed how we, as American Christians, came to understand Christianity. Our understanding of the purpose of the Gospel was altered. Today evangelicals conceive the Gospel largely as a "get-out-of-hell-free card" for sinners. It is a threshold moment that ushers you into a spiritual subculture. This is why we can't quite grasp how the Gospel might relate to Christians on a continual basis. The Gospel's saving effect is a preliminary event in our minds, but not constant. We are in the habit of looking back on it fondly. It's that moment we became Christians. God was gracious to get us in and we'll take it from here. This is one of the main reasons why our evangelical Christianity leaves individuals struggling for assurance and always feeling as if more needs to be done. The fact is, the American Gospel was not designed to create assurance. It was designed to create the absence of it. Otherwise, no one would ever be "converted." Our collective religion is about getting people in, but it has little to say about how they remain there.

One-Third Pietists

We are also part *pietists*. OK, another distinction has to be made at this point. Piety and pietism are (also) two altogether different realities. Piety is the God-caused transformation of the Christian's heart and life through the sanctifying work of the Holy Spirit aided by ordinary means. It is Spirit-wrought godliness. The latter, pietism, is a form of Christian practice that is focused mainly on the individual Christian's spiritual experience. As a rule, its major focus is the interior of the Christian life. This is compared to an emphasis on the objective realities of Christ's work found within reformed confessionalism. In other words, pietism is a Christian construct concerned about improving the moral and spiritual condition of the individual. To put it bluntly, it is mainly about Christians. Look around you. This is where you live. There are militant forms of pietism found in the polyester theology of fundamentalism. Here the emphasis is progressive morality. Or, on the other end of the pietistic spectrum, there are more popular and therapeutic forms. Anytime a sermon sounds like a self-help course and preacher sounds like a life-coach, you're on this end of things. Despite the extreme and obvious differences in these two brands of pietism, they have one thing that binds them together; they are mainly concerned about how the individual lives. The fundamentalist wants to make sure you're behaving. The pragmatist wants to make sure you're flourishing. Different tones. Same focus—the life of the Christian.

Not long after the Reformation a tedious and drawn out theological debate occurred within German Lutheranism over many number of issues. Disputations, as they were known, were common practice among the clergy. The pulpit was more or less a scholar's desk. The pendulum had swung in the direction of hyper-orthodoxy and away from the initial personal effects of the Reformation. The Christian life was largely unaddressed. This focus created a distance between the clergy and laity. It put the practical truths of Scripture out of the hands of ordinary people. The combination of these and other factors led to nominalism within the Church. People attended church because that's what German Protestants do.

Many prominent leaders of the time bemoaned the condition of the Lutheran state church and sought to change it. The Church needed to recapture the vital spiritual experience of the individual. To accomplish this they began to introduce elements of medieval mysticism back into common Christian practice. They wanted to replace hyper-orthodoxy with inner spiritualism and an "applied Christianity." This is the moment pietism was born. Pietism is by nature a reaction to the extremes of confessional theology and the Church's negligence of spirituality. In the pietist's eyes sacramentalism and confessionalism were to blame for the condition of the Church. As a result, the confessional standards of the Church were largely ignored. The pendulum was pushed back in the opposite direction. Individual experience rather than orthodoxy was the central focus of the pietists. Pietism, wherever it ends up, carries with it elements of quietism (Christian mysticism), legalism, and separatism. Our modern idea of "personal holiness" finds its origins here, as does our penchant for obsessive spirituality, our modern concepts of "devotions" and a "devotional life," and our practice of spiritual disciplines. By contrast, we might say reformed confessionalism emphasizes the objective realities of the work of Christ, and pietism emphasize subjective experiences of the individual Christian. The theology of the Reformation pointed *out* to Christ. The theology of pietism pointed *in* to the Christian.

Eventually, pietism became a formidable movement in Germany. Some branches of pietism were mystical in the extreme. There were plenty of fanatical heretics to go around. Others were more moderate. But, the core tenets of experience and spirituality remained at the heart of the phenomenon. Books were written. Colleges were founded. Philipp Jakob Spener, the father of pietism, wrote *Pia Desideria*, crystallizing the practical and experiential elements of Christianity. This one book gave the movement an identity. His writings, along with those of others, influenced numbers of spiritual leaders and denominations as it spread to other regions and countries. This includes key figures within the revivals of early America. John Wesley, for example, was directly influenced by pietistic theology. This can be seen in his emphasis on perfectionism and holiness. Pietism and the "holiness movement" were a match made in heaven.

The individualism of the American political scene and the breakdown of confessional influence created the perfect soil for pietism to take root. And it did take root. Immediately. From the very beginning evangelicalism has been a pietistic movement. Pietism, along with these other major influences, created a culture so innate in evangelicalism, most cannot fathom an alternative to the practice of Christianity other than the one characterized by hyper-spirituality and experience. But there is an alternative.

Making the Transition

I was in an airport walking down one of those long corridors that connect terminals—the ones with the moving sidewalks. I was behind an elderly couple that decided to take advantage of the technology. Why walk when you can ride? I was right behind them. As the husband stepped onto the belt, despite the recorded voice warning him about the impending movement, he stumbled and dropped a bag as he climbed aboard. Some stereotypical grumbling ensued which was met by his wife's observation of the obvious: "The lady told you to watch out." The old guy steadied himself and grabbed the rail. We eventually made it to the other end of the belt. Same voice. Same warning. Same results. The elderly man could not quite navigate the transition from the moving sidewalk onto the unmoving ground. He got in his own head. He choked. The belt more or less spit him out onto the carpet. He staggered and dropped his bag again. I swerved to miss him as I disembarked. There was more grumbling and the same retort from his amused wife. Bags were retrieved and they headed toward the down escalator to baggage claim. I did not stick around to see if he survived it.

The transition from pietism to confessionalism is very much like that scene. It can be hard to navigate. When we move from the flow of evangelicalism to the flow of a reformed-confessional world the change is abrupt. It can feel as if things have come to a screeching halt. It takes you a while to get your "sea legs." It's a very different sort of pace. When you are used to the perpetual motion of evangelical Christianity, rest seems odd. It takes some getting used to. You'll have to drop some baggage to make the transition.

Motivation: Delight Not Dread

One of the more profound adjustments concerns our motivation for obedience. Because dread is the resting heart rate of the fallen human being we typically do what we do out of fear, even as Christians. Mainly we have been driven forward by a church culture that has tapped into a sense of God's displeasure. Whether you know it or not, you've been running *from* something. We're hard-wired to run and hide.

> *Then the eyes of both were opened, and they knew that they were naked. And they sewed fig leaves together and made themselves loincloths. And they heard the sound of the LORD God walking in the garden in the cool of the day, and the man and his wife hid themselves from the presence of the LORD God among the trees of the garden. (Genesis 3:7-8)*

This switch is where things get really complicated. The hardest thing to do is to turn around and start running *toward* the thing you've been conditioned to run *from*. But, this is exactly what you need to do. This is exactly what the Gospel compels you to do.

> *Whoever is under the law … is not only under condemnation, but he is of necessity under a legal or slavish spirit. What he does, he does as a slave, to escape punishment. But he who is under grace, who is gratuitously accepted of God, and restored*

to his favour, is under a filial spirit. The principle of obedience in him is love, and not fear. Here, as everywhere else in the Bible, it is assumed that the favour of God is our life. We must be reconciled to him before we can be holy; we must feel that he loves us before we can love him. Paul says it was the love of Christ to him that constrained him to live for Him who thus loved him and gave Himself for him. The only hope therefore of sinners, is in freedom from the law, freedom from its condemnation, freedom from the obligation to fulfill it as the condition of acceptance, and freedom from its spirit. Those who are thus free, who renounce all dependence on their own merit or strength, who accept the offer of justification as a free gift of God, and who are assured that God for Christ's sake is reconciled to them, are so united to Christ that they partake of his life, and their holiness here and salvation hereafter are rendered perfectly certain.

Generally, our sense of dread comes and goes in greater or lesser degrees throughout our lives as Christians. There is nothing to fear, but we fear nonetheless. It's an instinct we live with until this life is done. What Luther called "the suspicion of God." This tension is part of what it means to be Protestant. We'll speak more to this later, but this struggle only exists where grace exists.

Suffice it to say, there are two ways you can manage this conflict and the underlying sense of dread. You can work the evangelical system. You can try to outrun it by becoming the type of person God would be proud to save. Or, on the other hand, you can stop, admit you're unworthy and throw yourself on the mercy of God. You can believe His promise that He accepts you right now—even in your inadequacies—through faith in Christ alone. Or, to put that more simply, you can rest. Those are your only options. He *might be* good with you. Or, He *is* good with you. That's it. Evangelicalism specializes in the former. The reformed confessional faith specializes in the latter. The shift here is complicated.

Normally, drawing out this contrast (running or resting) creates consternation in specific segments of the evangelical church. This is especially true of fundamentalism where life is lived under a cloud of doubt. This mindset can't conceive of another way of living. Salvation is more or less viewed as a journey across thin ice where the sound of cracking keeps us running for the shore. The specific concern has to do with the incentive for good works. Because we've been conditioned to believe our acceptance before God is dependent on the type of person we are at any given time, the concept of rest sounds like a compromise. The basic fear is that stressing assurance of God's good pleasure through faith alone will result in the lack of activity in the Christian life. Obviously, *sola fide* is a bone in the throat of pietism because it fears an emphasis on justification by grace through faith will only result in a moral laxity. If we assure people they are safe regardless of personal progress they will never progress. This is a fundamental difference in how the reformed and pietistic systems view the Christian life. (It's ironic that this was the same charge the Roman Catholic Church levied against the reformers.) In evangelicalism there is never a thought that another and wholly different motivation for our pilgrimage exists. Who would ever believe that our lives as Christians might be propelled along by acceptance, rather than by threat or doubt? But, there *are* better reasons to obey than you've been given. Our lives should be driven by delight, not dread.

For many, this description of the Christian life is nothing more than a contemporary strategy for avoiding spiritual rigor—a soft sort of Christianity. "Easy believism" as it is known on the street. But, historically speaking, it's an old idea and the original one. Assurance was the ultimate takeaway of the reformation. Resting in His promises is synonymous with what it means to have faith.

> *Those whom God effectually calls, He also freely justifies; not by infusing righteousness into them, but by pardoning their sins, and by accounting and accepting their persons as righteous; not for any thing wrought in them, or done by them, but for Christ's sake alone; nor by imputing faith itself, the act of believing, or any other evangelical obedience to them, as their righteousness; but by imputing the obedience*

*and satisfaction of Christ unto them, **they receiving and resting on Him and His righteousness by faith; which faith they have not of themselves, it is the gift of God.***

*Faith, thus **receiving and resting on Christ and His righteousness**, is the alone instrument of justification: yet is it not alone in the person justified, but is ever accompanied with all other saving graces, and is no dead faith, but works by love.*

That is very specific language. Stop and think about what is being said. First of all, the idea of "infusing righteousness" was essential to a system of self-reformation. Saints cooperated with a grace that was infused into them through the Church. Christians cooperated with that grace and moved along a scale of acceptance (justification) through works of penance. Salvation was subjective, linear, and open-ended. Protestantism rejected this construct outright. God justified the sinner not by offering an opportunity, but "by pardoning their sins, and by accounting and accepting their persons as righteous." It is an act of God's grace. Saving faith itself is defined here as "resting and receiving." Resting, therefore, is the posture of the regenerate heart before God. But this rest does not result in negligence. Rather, it "is ever accompanied with all other saving graces, and is no dead faith." This obedience is not derived from a sense of fear and doubt, but "are works by love."

Needless to say, *why we do what we do* is one spot the evangelical-pietistic and reformed-confessional worlds clash. But resting and moving are not at odds in the Gospel. In a reformed framework they happen concurrently and depend one upon the other. We rest as we persevere. We persevere even as we rest. Our rest is the source of our perseverance. We repent even as we trust. We fight against our sin even as we rely completely (by faith) on something outside of us. This has been the emphasis of the reformed church from the very beginning. As to whether an emphasis on faith, perseverance, and assurance leads to moral laxity and inactivity, consider the *Cannons of Dort*:

> *Having set forth the orthodox teaching, the Synod* **rejects the errors of those who teach that the teaching of the assurance of perseverance and of salvation is by its very nature and character an opiate of the flesh and is harmful to godliness, good morals, prayer, and other holy exercises,** *but that, on the contrary, to have doubt about this is praiseworthy.*
>
> *For these people show that they do not know the effective operation of God's grace and the work of the indwelling Holy Spirit, and they contradict the apostle John, who asserts the opposite in plain words: "Dear friends, now we are children of God, but what we will be has not yet been made known. But we know that when he is made known, we shall be like*

him, for we shall see him as he is. Everyone who has this hope in him purifies himself, just as he is pure" (1 John 3:2-3). Moreover, they are refuted by the examples of the saints in both the Old and the New Testament, who though assured of their perseverance and salvation yet were constant in prayer and other exercises of godliness.

Our suspicion of a delight-driven existence is evidence of how far we've drifted from the center of the good news. Without realizing it, our construct for the Christian life is set against the orthodox definition of justification.

Our confusion here can be observed in a number of places. Consider Christian liberty. Normally, when evangelicals think of Christian liberty they think about ethics. Popularly, Christian liberty is the discussion about what we are free (or not free) to participate in. (Think alcohol and movies.) True. There are ethical outworkings, but the primary point in the discussion of Christian liberty concerns our relationship to God. Christian liberty is a synonym for the effects of justification. We have been set free from the severe and eternal consequences of being a sinner before a Holy God. We are free from our guilt, shame, and the deserved condemnation. Because of the work of Christ we have no reason to fear. We are free to go. No one is coming to get us. We will not be condemned in the future no matter how deeply we know we deserve to be. Consider the following explanation from the *Westminster Confession of Faith*:

> *The liberty which Christ has purchased for believers under the Gospel consists **in their freedom from the guilt of sin, and condemning wrath of God, the curse of the moral law; and, in their being delivered from this present evil world, bondage to Satan, and dominion of sin; from the evil of afflictions, the sting of death, the victory of the grave, and everlasting damnation; as also, in their free access to God, and their yielding obedience unto Him, not out of slavish fear, but a child-like love and willing mind.** All which were common also to believers under the law. But, under the New Testament, the liberty of Christians is further enlarged, in their freedom from the yoke of the ceremonial law, to which the Jewish Church was subjected; and in greater boldness of access to the throne of grace, and in fuller communications of the free Spirit of God, than believers under the law did ordinarily partake of.*
>
> *God alone is Lord of the conscience, and has left it free from the doctrines and commandments of men, which are, in any thing, contrary to His Word; or beside it, if matters of faith, or worship. **So that, to believe such doctrines, or to obey such commands, out of conscience, is to betray true liberty of conscience:***

and the requiring of an implicit faith, and an absolute and blind obedience, is to destroy liberty of conscience, and reason also.

Robbing Christians of their freedom is not primarily about legalistically restricting their participation in certain activities. Rather, it is when we pull them back under the dread of condemnation from which Christ liberated them, by offering moralism rather than grace. It is to bring them back under bondage by delivering a message that erodes their confidence in the Gospel—turning one's faith back upon the person rather than Christ. All this to say, when doubt and dread are used as stimuli for Christian obedience, we are assailing the benefits of Christ's works applied to the Christian. We are opposed to the sufficiency of His work by suggesting something else is needed in reconciling us to God. In stark contrast to this, the confession states that in Christ we are granted "free access to God" and we do not obey Him out of "slavish fear" but through a "childlike love and willing mind." We obey out of delight and not dread. To do otherwise is to refuse the Christian the benefits of Christ. "Therefore, since we have been justified by faith we have peace with God through our Lord Jesus Christ" (Romans 5:1).

Clarity: Law and Gospel

"What's that?" I asked. I was being nosy. My friend was showing a group of people a video on her phone. It was that all too recognizable scene where people are gathered around a four-by-two-inch glass screen held out at arm's length. By the time I got around into view, the video was paused on a frame of her dad. He was wiping tears from his eyes. He's a giant of a man. So a shot of him in tears did not match his persona. "This is my dad at his birthday party. We took him out to lunch and gave him a pair of color-blindness-corrective glasses. He's been color-blind his whole life. This is his reaction to seeing color for the first time. Watch this." I had never heard of this. She was replaying it for me, but those who just watched were watching it again. I quickly discovered why. So, he opens the package, takes out the glasses, receives an explanation and puts them on. Immediately (and I mean instantaneously), he snatches them off his head and tears up. He looks up tearfully at his family with sincere gratitude plastered on his face and says, "This is what you guys see?" This is followed by spontaneous applause and the video returns to that frame of her dad in tear-filled amazement. I was in tears too. Turns out these videos are all over the internet. Surprising unsuspecting people trapped in a world of grey with the beauty of color is a real thing.

Having people look upon God's Word through the lenses of Law and Gospel is very much like seeing it in color for the first time. Without this necessary distinction, the world of the Bible comes to us in an ashen gray of tedious moralism. Everything is in one shade of bleak. It all reads in a monochromatic: "Do this and live." When you put on Gospel spectacles, that changes. Hope comes into focus. That hopeless gray which tinted our perspective, suddenly becomes the backdrop by which the full color of the Gospel pops off the page. The Bible becomes a sort of theological art gallery where you wander the halls beholding stories anew, now captured in pure light. You sit and stare at paintings of redemption that you've seen countless times, once muted by shadows. I'm not overstating things here. Once you see it you can never un-see it. I guarantee that you will say the same thing my friend's dad said, "This is what you guys see?" It's overwhelming to look upon the Gospel in full color when it has been hidden from view by the mixture Law and Gospel.

Law and Gospel are two great threads running through the Bible. The Law is threat, judgment, demand, obligation, and condemnation. The Gospel is promise, mercy, grace, and redemption. In the first we are required to do but cannot. In the latter we are given and not required. The Law is duty. The Gospel is gift. The Law is non-saving and the Gospel is. The Gospel is not condemning but the Law is. These threads emerge from the beginning. "The man and the woman hid themselves" (Law), and "He shall bruise your head" (Gospel). Both threat and promise remain until the end:

> *Blessed are those who wash their robes, so that they may have the right to the tree of life and that they may enter the city by the gates* (Gospel). *Outside are the dogs and sorcerers and the sexually immoral and murderers and idolaters, and everyone who loves and practices falsehood* (Law). *(Revelation 22:14-15)*

The Law and the Gospel are two different messages to mankind. The Gospel is a surprise announcement. The Law is a redundant verdict of guilty. The Gospel is "good news" primarily because the Law carries such a devastating declaration. The Law is like the "red-flag" surf warning at the beach. It is sufficient to point out the danger, but powerless to help the drowning victim. It will never dive in and save you from the undertow. It will only stand there and watch you go under. The Gospel comes to us in our despair and drags us back to shore. It is the good news of rescue.

This distinction went missing in my early Christian experience. My understanding of the Gospel was muddled. It was a combination of "do" and "done." What a friend of mine calls "glawspel." There was a permanent and underlying suggestion that my acceptance before God in the future depended partly on my contribution in the present. It was like a rock in my shoe. I could never fully stand on the promises of God. I had no idea what my struggle was until someone handed me the right spectacles and said, "Here put these on." Then I saw it. The distinctions between Law and Gospel were suddenly everywhere. I saw two threads like parallel tracks emerging from the beginning and extending past me out into eternity—one condemning and the other saving. One standing there like "Captain Obvious" watching me drown in my sin and yelling, "Swim harder!" The other was doing a swan dive of grace, unconditionally swimming out to me and rescuing me from my peril. The relief was overwhelming. So was the sense of betrayal. In my journey, the colors of the Gospel were kept from my weary eyes. The need for the Gospel came flooding into view. So did the confusion all around me.

I was told rather consistently, for example, that the rich young ruler remained in his sin because he was unwilling to do what Jesus asked of him. Had he been willing to liquidate his holdings and distribute them to his neighbor he would have been saved. By extension, I was also told this is our responsibility to the lost. Our message to them is simple. They must be willing to give up everything and follow Jesus in order to be saved. But subtly, repentance was redefined as a renovation of life that warranted the acceptance of Christ. But this is not a biblical definition of repentance. Without really understanding what was happening, I was offered a definition of salvation that depended on the will of man, rather than the will of God. In this construct the human heart can only despair. Moralism was the net effect.

In its confusion the Church rather consistently speaks out of both sides of its theological mouth and points us back to Rome. A primary reason is because we don't make the distinction between Law and Gospel. We end up taking the Law's absolute demands and relativizing them. That's exactly what we do with the rich young ruler. We describe something as possible, which is clearly impossible because we can't see the starkness of the Law. Jesus was speaking in absolute terms. The Law is not a suggestion. It is impossible to save oneself through the works of the Law. There's no way Jesus is suggesting this. In reality, Jesus was doing the opposite. He was driving this man to despair of his own works. He was holding the moralist's heart beneath the water line of the Law's unrelenting demands long enough for him to come up gasping for grace. Sadly, the young man walked away holding his breath. But it was his failure before the Law in this moment that made the need for Jesus obvious. Now as I sit beneath this portrait of the Rich Young ruler it appears to me as a task I need not to complete in order for Christ to accept me. Rather, it is a vivid full-color portrait of the hopelessness of men to save themselves. Standing in beautiful relief is man's only hope: Jesus.

Both Law and Gospel should be preached where they are found. The Law itself is good and holy. "The law of the Lord is perfect" (Psalm 19:7). But, due to our fallen condition, a perfect conformity to it is impossible, and perfect conformity is what it demands. Yet we should not hesitate in allowing the Law to expose those inadequacies and shortcomings in our lives as believers (diagnosis). This is the Law's role in us. But, we should never imply that the Law saves, or changes. Nor should we imply that the condemnation inherent in the Law affects our standing before God. It does not. It only exposes that which has already been dealt with on the cross. (Romans 8:1).

> *The law uncovers sin; it makes the sinner guilty and sick; indeed, it proves him to be under condemnation … The gospel offers grace and forgives sin; it cures the sickness and leads to salvation.*

We should not hesitate to offer the unconditional accomplishment of God in Christ on our behalf—the Gospel of Grace. And, we should never imply that the Gospel is something to do. Ultimately, the Gospel has the last word. The Law, while it might bark its commands at us, has no jurisdiction over us. Romans 6:14 tells us we are no longer under law, but under grace. The resurrection ended the Law's dominion. The Law can tell us to do something (and be accurate) but it can neither help us to do it, nor punish us for not doing it perfectly. We're free. So says the Gospel.

The Law of God should be swung unrelentingly as a great hammer that crushes and dismembers all futile attempts at self-justification, all speculations that we might gain a right standing before God by our own means—or by any other means outside of faith in the merits of Christ—and favorable views of our own condition. The Law is the bad news for the unrighteous. It should also be wielded with unyielding and unmixed liberty at the heart of the redeemed. That is, it should not be relativized to appear as a means for transformation, but presented in all its purity as a diagnostic of our utter failure to comply with the absolute standard of God. In this there should be two results. First, all those delicate contours of needed change in our hearts are exposed, allowing us to confess that true means of transformation and conformity is resident only in the Spirit's renovating power. For the Law cannot change us. It can only expose our need for it. Second, the Law, while landing its blows against the reality of our sin, should send us (the redeemed) fleeing not to ourselves, but to the shelter of the One who bore the penalty of the Law on our behalf—Christ.

In all of this, it should not be assumed that the Law and the Gospel are essentially opposed to one another. As one theologian noted, "The Reformed have always recognized that, however antithetical law and gospel are to sinners, they are not antithetical to God." The mystery of redemption remains in this: The God who demanded justice with His creatures (Law) saved those same unworthy creatures by meeting the demands of His justice Himself (Gospel). The tension of the Law and Gospel remains as the same foolishness of the Cross that Paul spoke of in 1 Corinthians 1:18.

Life: Faith vs. Faithfulness

The breakthrough moment for Martin Luther—when he understood righteousness as a gift rather than a personal accomplishment—is known as his "tower experience." He was in the Black Cloister Tower in Wittenberg where his Augustinian order was boarded. He was in his room wrestling with Romans 1:17: "For therein is revealed a righteousness of God from faith unto faith: as it is written, but the righteous shall live by faith." Here's the moment of clarity in his own words.

I greatly longed to understand Paul's epistle to the Romans and nothing stood in the way but that one expression "the righteousness of God," because I took it to mean that righteousness whereby God is just and deals justly in punishing the unjust.

My situation was that, although an impeccable monk, I stood before God as a sinner troubled in conscience, and I had no confidence that my merit would assuage Him. Therefore I did not love a just angry God, but rather hated and murmured against Him. Yet I clung to the dear Paul and had a great yearning to know what he meant.

Night and day I pondered until I saw the connection between the righteousness of God and the statement that "the just shall live by faith." Then I grasped that the righteousness of God is that righteousness by which through grace and sheer mercy God justifies us through faith. Thereupon I felt myself to be reborn and to have gone through open doors into paradise. There a totally other face of the entire Scripture showed itself to me. Thereupon I ran through the Scriptures from memory. I also found in other terms an analogy, as, the work of God, that is, what God does in us, the power of God, with which he makes us strong, the wisdom of God, with which he makes us wise, the strength of God, the salvation of God, the glory of God.

It's hard to overestimate the historic impact of this moment. Nothing has been the same since the monk saw what he saw. To Protestants this is a memorial of the Gospel's recovery. Some of us know it by heart. But, there's something in his comments that is often passed over. It's his description of the Gospel's immediate impact on his understanding of the Bible.

> *There **a totally other face of the entire Scripture** showed itself to me. Thereupon I ran through the Scriptures from memory. I also found in other terms an analogy, as, **the work of God**, that is, what God does in us, the power of God, with which he makes us strong, the wisdom of God, with which he makes us wise, the strength of God, the salvation of God, the glory of God.*

His point is obvious. The Gospel completely transformed his understanding of Scripture. No longer was it a recounting of the *faithfulness of man to God*, but rather it was about the *faithfulness of God in saving men*. Not man in pursuit of God, but God in pursuit of man. What he calls, "the work of God." Stated simply the story is about faith (in God) and not faithfulness (of man) to God. The moment this occurred to Luther, the Scripture turned around and headed in an opposite direction. It's like that classic scene where the growth chart in the business presentation is upside down. Apparently, the business is in financial crisis. People panic. And then, "Oh, sorry." The chart is righted and arrows head upwards.

Things are great, actually. Everyone breathes a sigh of relief. That was Luther's experience. The indicators were always bleak; arrows were always pointing to a deficit. There was no way to turn it around. And then he noticed he was reading it "upside down." *Sola fide* turned it right-side up. It was good news, actually. Not the bad news he had always encountered. He had read the chart wrong. Once he turned it over, he began to see the Gospel reality everywhere. That's what he means by "analogy." It was all about "God's work" and not ours.

Before this moment the Bible was suffocating—mankind trapped under the impossible standard of God's righteousness, gasping for breath. Faith and faithfulness were mixed together. No wonder Luther was angry with God and saw Him as his enemy. He was locked in a medieval *Groundhog Day*, waking up in the same despair, reliving the same failure over and over with no way out. He read it as our faithfulness to God, but not as His faithfulness to us. And then he stepped out of that hopelessness "through open doors into paradise." You can understand why Luther was so elated. Can you imagine how we would feel if we discovered that we had interpreted the Bible wrongly our entire life? Sure we can. Many of us have had our own tower experience. We read it differently now. It's not about us. It is about Him. Our modern interpretive model is only a milder version of Luther's before his clarity, but it yields and focuses on the same thing— *our faithfulness*. As far as we know, the Bible's plot line is mainly about us, and what we should be doing. It is far less about what

God did on our behalf. This is not hard to prove.

Consider the passage Luther was wrestling with in Romans, "the righteous shall live by faith." What does this passage mean? The way we've been conditioned, we most likely read it this way: "Righteous people are those who live faithful lives." Or, we take it to mean righteous people are characterized by faithfulness. It's about how we live. Our faithfulness. We can look back in the Old Testament, for example, and see faithful people who rise to the level of an honorable mention. But, this interpretation is impossible given the context of Romans, not to mention the whole of the Bible. Paul was arguing against this very thing in his discourse on justification. "Righteousness" in Paul's argument is not a relative thing. It is not a reference to the quality of our faith. "Righteousness" is absolute. "But now the righteousness of God has been manifested apart from the law, although the Law and the Prophets bear witness to it" (Romans 3:21a). Absolute righteousness is what God demands of mankind. But, this is impossible for sinners. The "good news" is that this righteousness is given to us as a gift through faith. "The righteousness of God through faith in Jesus Christ for all who believe" (Romans 3:21b). The only way the attainment of righteousness is possible is through faith.

Ultimately, Romans 1:17 is a preface to the argument of the letter—the necessity of imputed righteousness. Those who are righteous are righteous by faith, not by works. They are accepted by God now and shall be accepted by God in the future by faith alone. It is not by any work or quality in their persons. It has always been this way, "from faith for faith." To conclude otherwise would be to contradict Paul's thesis on the Gospel. Luther had translated it as we normally do, "righteousness through faithfulness." His *aha* moment came when he understood it to mean "righteousness through faith." Faith (in God) and faithfulness (a quality in us) are very different realities. As it concerns our standing before God, faithfulness can only lead to despair. But, faith in His promises brings rest to the weary pilgrim.

The same observation can be made concerning Galatians 2:20: "I have been crucified with Christ. It is no longer I who live, but Christ who lives in me. **And the life I now live in the flesh I live by faith** in the Son of God, who loved me and gave himself for me." We miss what Paul is saying here. Paul doesn't mean that his life is now lived *faithfully*, or that his day-to-day existence is fueled by the *quality* of his faith. Paul is contrasting his previous life as a Pharisee with his present life in Christ. Before, his standing *before* God was dependent on his faithfulness *to* God. That was his life. But the life he "now lives in the flesh" is lived by faith "in the Son of God." His standing before God is dependent on Christ's faithfulness to him. His faith *in* Christ. Not his faithfulness *to* Christ. This is why he concludes as he does describing the work of Christ, "who loved me and gave himself for me." It all depends on the benefits of Christ. Faith not faithfulness.

Perspective: Pain and Not Triumph

The most expensive bottle of wine to sell at auction sold on December 5, 1985, for around one hundred and fifty thousand dollars. One bottle. It was one of the mystical "Jefferson Bottles" dating back the eighteenth century. History records that as a diplomat to France, Thomas Jefferson developed an obsession with French wine, especially Lafitte Bordeaux. In modern currency he spent nearly one hundred and eighty thousand dollars of his own money on French wines. Two hundred years later, somewhere in Paris, a dozen or so dusty bottles of wine were discovered behind a brick wall in a basement. Written on the bottles was the inscription: *1787 Lafitte Th.J.* After some research and science it was determined that the bottles were indeed authentic and in superb condition. When the gavel fell at auction the bottle was gone in minutes.

Not surprisingly after the Jefferson bottle was discovered and sold at auction, other Jefferson bottles started appearing. Wealthy enthusiasts lined up to purchase them. The industrialist Bill Koch bought four bottles for five hundred thousand dollars—the most money spent on wine in the history of wine auctions. A few days later he received a phone call suggesting that the bottles were counterfeit but in nearly every other way they appeared to be authentic. So Koch hired some scientists to test it. They tested the wine for a specific isotope, Carbon 14. Carbon 14 is a radioactive isotope that exists in non-lethal levels in everything. But, after 1950, as a result of U.S. nuclear testing, the level of Carbon 14 in the atmosphere went up substantially. When the bottles were tested for the isotope they came back with post-1950 levels. In other words, due to a high concentration of a nearly imperceptible element, the bottles were proven to be fake.

If you tested the spirituality of evangelicalism, the nearly imperceptible element that permeates it and exists in abnormally high post-enlightenment levels, would be triumphalism. Within Christian theology triumphalism is the latent expectation of victory and progress in the here and now. Or, to put that in more colloquial terminology, American Evangelical Christianity is infused with the concept of personal success and advancement. All things in our Christian world must progress and move forward to be authentic and useful. If we are not progressing and moving forward, then something must be wrong with our faith. If our churches are not large and cutting edge something is wrong with our church. On and on it goes. Triumphalism is the atmospheric fallout of the enlightenment where man became center and his improvement inevitable. Humanism seeped into our Christianity. Triumphalism exists in the more extreme forms such as the health, wealth, and prosperity teachings. These are obvious counterfeits of biblical Christianity. But what's harder to detect is the presence of triumphalism in the more acceptable versions of our Christian practice. But it is there. Triumphalism is the pressure we sense at our backs ready to run us down should we delay in advancement, or stumble for even a moment. Essentially, in our contexts anything that reeks of weakness or failure is automatically categorized as an impediment to spiritual progress. Our Christianity follows the motto: "If you're not moving forward, you're moving backward." Ironically, Jesus preached a contradictory message. "The greatest among you shall be your servant. Whoever exalts himself will be humbled, and whoever humbles himself will be exalted" (Matthew 23:11-12).

For Martin Luther it is the difference between a theology of glory and a theology of the Cross. A theology of glory is basic triumphalism. Our Christian experience over the whole of our life advances in a series of increasing victories and personal progression. This trajectory is based on the reality that Jesus' resurrection ushered in a new era where the effects and dominion of sin are being rolled back. All things are available to us for a victorious Christian life. There is no reason we should not be getting better. If we are properly working the means at our disposal and performing as required, we can only improve. A theology of the Cross, like a theology of glory, also recognizes the dominion-defeating event of the resurrection, but by contrast it maintains a more realistic view of our pilgrimage in this new aeon. Life is filled with suffering and toil all the way up until the end. Our life experience is emblematic of the Cross, because God works in weakness.

For Luther, the Cross transforms our understanding about God and life. The Cross turns our built-in perception of life on its head. If the Cross is the revelation of the nature of God to man then who can doubt that we have misunderstood God and the nature of His kingdom? In the Cross, everything is turned upside down (or right-side up, depending on how you see it). What we conceive as power in our culture is actually weakness in God's kingdom. What we conceive as wisdom in our institutions is actually foolishness in God's counsel. Death is life. Failure is victory. Basically, whatever mankind most values is of no value in the kingdom of God. It is not hard to see how the American work ethic infused into our evangelical spirituality is a contradiction of the very nature of the Christian faith. Our life is one of striving against the headwind of life, not the tailwind of triumphalism.

What Luther pointed to as the norm for the Christian experience was the suffering and weakness displayed in the Cross of Christ. What appears to be an utter defeat and humiliation before men is actually the power and victory of God on display. For us, therefore, we can expect that God will work in, through, and around us not so much in great victories, but in moments of intense pain and suffering. That's how God works in our lives. He's in the whirlwind. To expect that our lives will eventually be free of the pain and discomfort of our condition, is to deny the Cross itself. To expect that one day in this life we will get past the gravitational pull of our corruption is a false notion. Life is a battleground, not a playground. Pain, failure, weakness, foolishness, and conflict are how God does what He does. Sorrow and hardship, not victory and advancement, are the norms in our experience, not the exception. To view the Christian life otherwise is to mix the Gospel with the isotope of American triumphalism.

Is there any victory to be expected for us? Of course there is. But it does not look like the victory of men. It is a victory similar to that of the Cross. It certainly does not result in an ever-increasing spiritual self-confidence. Nor is it the expectation that we will one day get clear of our earthly struggles. Victory for the Christian is the exact opposite: the absence of personal confidence and constant struggling. Victory comes when our personal powers are completely defeated and we throw ourselves entirely on the power of God, when we are reduced to a child-like trust in the promises of God, and when everything we trust (power, wealth, influence, status, possessions) is stripped away through pain. Christianity is a religion for losers not because we promote defeatism or self-loathing, but because losing *is* winning.

Let me give you an example of how triumphalism affects us on a daily basis. Think about the theology of the Cross in light of how we evaluate churches in America. What is a successful church in our culture? One that is growing in numbers disproportionate to those around it? Or, one that has tapped into the culture around it and draws people in? Or one that has implemented the most recent church methodology and is bursting at the seams? Whether we want to admit it or not, we measure the success of churches based on size, newness, or the hype around them. If it's a "thriving church" then we can rest assured that God is at work there. These are the types of churches American Christians are drawn to because that's what American Christians value— big personalities and innovative ministries. But God has never worked this way, not in any normative sense. He always works through the insignificant, marginalized, and powerless. Like the Cross, He is always where you least expect Him to be. This is because we see things upside down from how they truly are. The mega-church is merely a shrine to triumphalism. The endless stream of instruction is nothing more than a modern theology of glory applied to the modern Christian.

Think about this on the personal level. Triumphalism is the reason that failure and struggle seem so out of place in our churches. This is the reason we've no patience for people caught in extended struggles. This is why we hand average people principles to dislodge their lives from the ordinary. It's the reason "mediocre" is a curse word in our contexts. We have no value for weakness or personal hardship. *"Those people should have known better."* But, this is exactly how God works in His people. This is the reason "broken" people feel out of place in the average church. It is also the reason the better people are actually broken people hiding behind facades. How can there be hope for the weary soul when the value system in our churches measures everything in progress and performance? You know what? Life is hard. Really hard. Sometimes it flows backward and not forward. Sometimes faithful Christians experience life-altering disasters deep into life. Christians suffer disproportionately in all sorts of ways. Christian marriages break down. Christians have lifelong bouts of depression and anxiety. Christians experience financial ruin due to bad choices. Christians battle addictions. Christian kids rebel against Christian parents. We're human beings weighed down with all sorts of maladies. None of this is an excuse for misbehavior. It's reality.

CHAPTER THREE

The Weary Pilgrim

There was this elderly man in my church affectionately known as "Colonel." He had a long and illustrious career as a colonel in the U.S. Army. "Colonel" was not applied affectionately. It's what we called him because it's who he was. In every way he was a colonel—regimented, tough, demanding, straight talking. We would never dare to refer to him by his given name, Dave. Colonel is with the Lord now so I'm safe in using it here. Although, I did just look over my shoulder to make sure he wasn't sneaking up on me. Colonel was a baby boomer who grew up during the Great Depression. Which means he was "resourceful." He was one of tightest men I've ever met. He was on our deacon board and finance team at one point. The thought of buying anything new was unthinkable and un-American. When I was new to the church I proposed we purchase a new computer and projectors for the worship center. He nearly ordered a "code red" on me. The dude saved the leftover coffee we brewed each Sunday for use the following Sunday. "It's perfectly safe to consume," he would say. Think *rations*. He showed up early every Sunday to heat it up. All the yuppies rolled their eyes as they sipped their Starbucks. We didn't get all the fuss. Who rations coffee? Answer: Someone who remembers a time when he could not afford to buy it.

Colonel was like this because he experienced something most of us had not. The Depression was a horrific economic disaster. Banks collapsed. People lost their savings. Jobs were in limited supply. Incomes were cut in half overnight. In the worst of circumstances people were boiling leather shoes to eat. The average family faced severe financial strains. They pulled together in order to survive. Everyone was involved. Kids pitched in along with their parents. If you were out of diapers you were doing something to help. *Resourcefulness* was life. Nothing was wasted. Not even week-old coffee.

Most families with houses had a subsistence garden on their property where a majority of their food—albeit scarce—was produced. Colonel had one in his backyard that he worked on until the day he passed away. In fact, I think he passed away in his garden. But Colonel did not need a garden. By the time he passed away he was quite well off. But, that did not matter. His person had been shaped by the life-altering experience of financial catastrophe and the context of destitution. He took nothing for granted. I would go sit with Colonel and have a beer on his back porch from time to time. He would tell me about his childhood and how formative it was; how he learned to value the small things and minimize luxuries. Then he would lecture me about the excesses of our church budget. We did not get Colonel's coffee rations because we did not understand what he was responding to. We were too far removed. There was no apparent financial threat. But the more he described his experience to me, the more he drew me into his reality. I got it.

The experience with Colonel is similar to engaging the writings of the reformers and the confessional standards. To understand them you need to understand where the men were coming from. The writings are largely (nearly singularly) concerned that we understand the benefits of Christ, otherwise known as the Gospel. That is, they focus on the objective realities of redemption almost to the exclusion of subjective or practical ones. The Christian's experience is not completely absent, but it is minimal and always presented in light of greater reality. Unlike modern contributions to the Christian *corpus*, their works are almost exclusively about Christ and His work of redemption. The emphasis of their message lies mainly in faith (Christ as Savior) and not faithfulness (the Christian life). The confessions are particularly focused on the finer details of faith in Christ and all the corresponding particulars. As you read them you can sense that all the carefully crafted language is in reaction to something.

Something happened to make them like this. There was something that shaped their perception of the Christian message and life; something to which they had no intention of returning.

It was moralism. That's what lay behind their narrow and belligerent focus on sovereign grace. Generations had lived within a religion that placed all hope for redemption upon the feeble wills of sinful men. It was a pervasive darkness. There is no hope in moralism. It is damning and exhausting. Futile. When the light of the Gospel finally broke through in Luther's discovery countless saints were freed from its bondage. The good news of God's grace surfaced like the breaking dawn on a dark town. Hence Calvin's motto: *Post tenebras lux.* "After darkness light." The reaction of the Roman Catholic Church was harsh and immediate. The reformed Gospel was seen as heresy since it detached salvation from the church and bound it to faith alone. Rome still sees Protestantism as heresy.

Moralism had crushed the souls of average people for centuries. God was viewed mainly as a distant and mysterious tyrant. Christ Himself was viewed as an unsympathetic and harsh judge. This is where the mediation of Mary originated. She mediates not between men and God, but men and Christ, hence the reason Mary is always depicted as holding the infant Christ. She assuages his temper toward sinners. Given this view of the Almighty, if the Church told you that your only hope was personal penance and grace dispensed through the Church, that is what you would commit yourself to. And that's what the Church said.

To the people who had previously lived in these conditions *sola fide* was a radical notion. The most radical of all. The idea that sinful man was just before God through faith alone was against every fiber of their being. We don't really understand how earth shattering *sola fide* is because we weren't there. We're too far removed and take too much for granted. This is why I like talking with Roman Catholics about redemption. We're both talking about the same reality, but coming to different conclusions. They get it (what's at stake), albeit from the other side. I once had a series of conversations with a young Catholic lady who was visiting our church. At the end of our discourse she basically concluded that she could not convert to Protestantism because there was too much at stake. She could not let go of the Church and throw herself on the flimsy reality of faith alone. While I disagreed with her, I totally get that.

What you hear in the reformers are men using all of their theological and pastoral capacity to convince people conditioned otherwise that they could let go of the religious apparatus and throw themselves completely and wholly on Christ. He alone is sufficient to save outside of any quality in them, and/or any deed done by them. The reformers were not driving them to perform, but driving them from performance to Christ. They did not need to be convinced once of Christ's sufficiency, but constantly. Everything in them worked against faith. The closer you stand to the Reformation the more this makes sense. The farther away you stand, the more this emphasis seems superfluous. No reformer ever would have suggested that grace could be overemphasized. And no German or French peasants would have struggled to see the Gospel's relevance to their every breath. They rationed every last bit of the Gospel. For us the relevance and consistent propagation of objective theological categories seem a bit much—like rolling our eyes at a baby boomer rationing pots of coffee. "Move on to the relevant stuff," we say. To them the Gospel was the relevant stuff. We're simply too far away and conditioned otherwise to get it.

Let's Go Back

If we went back...back before this strange event we call Evangelicalism... back to the epicenter of Protestantism just as the light was dawning. If we went back, we would find a moment very similar to the present one. I don't mean this in a good way. If you pay attention you will begin to realize our experience as Evangelicals at present is similar to the one from which we were originally freed. Our theological commitments at present are the type that lead to the same sort of despair a medieval German peasant would have experienced. If assurance was the prize of the Reformation—and it was—then it is no stretch to suggest that we find ourselves back in a moment comparable to the one before it was rescued. There are differences between here and there. One major difference is the absence of any centralizing magisterium that imprisoned the common man to the instrumentality of the Church. But the decentralization of the modern church offers its own sort of bondage, found in an endless and confusing offering of opinions, over-spiritualized advice, and strategies for personal fulfillment. Though different in form, the two are not dissimilar in their results. It is a proven fact that the presence of limitless options in any culture will only lead to dissatisfaction and emptiness. The perpetual strategies for an improved spiritual self leave modern people just as exhausted as pre-modern ones. Evangelicalism is not the type of faith designed to provide the weary with assurances of God's good favor. In this we have become the same sort of oppressive force we once threw off. If this seems a stretch, simply consider the ethos in which you live your Christian life. It is an undeniable fact that nearly the entire emphasis of evangelical Christianity is concerned with the Christian and not Christ. There is very little emphasis on that which is outside of us and for us. All things point inward and to us. This is the point at which the two moments in history overlap. There are differences. In the sixteenth century, the real concern was mainly perdition. In the twenty-first century, the real concern is mainly performance. In either case, the result is despair.

The crisis at the Reformation occurred because someone started digging around in the archives of biblical Christianity. A monk went *ad fontes*, or back to the "original sources." He combed through the primary documents. To his surprise, they all pointed outward to God and not inward to man. As he compared his understanding to the teaching of the Apostle Paul, the failure of his religion was immediately apparent. When justification is leaned over on its side and viewed linearly we are doomed. It's impossible.

> *For in our age the temptation to presumption besets many, especially those who try with all their might to be just and good without knowing the righteousness of God, which is most bountifully and freely given us in Christ. They try to do good of themselves in order that they might stand before God clothed in their own virtues and merits. But this is impossible.*

In Luther's world, God's acceptance of the person, and the person's commitment to God were fused together in one unending act. Medieval Christianity was the original Church-sponsored self-improvement program. To be justified in Luther's time was to *participate* in a program of moral advancement offered by the Church. The message of Christianity was about how to become a better person through various material and ecclesiastical instruments, and how your commitment to these might get you home. Hope within this system was measured in degrees of improvement. Degrees of improvement were dependent on the commitment of the individual. It was an endless and hopeless loop of despair. If the requirement is total improvement (perfection), and it is, then anyone who cares to notice will realize the system is rigged. A finger is always on the scale.

It is in this way that evangelicalism bears a resemblance to that tortuous ambiguity of medieval theology. If we go *ad fontes*

—we will immediately see how far from the center we have drifted. Similarly, to be an evangelical Christian in our day is to commit oneself to a system of self-improvement. We speak mainly in first person (I, me) and rarely in third (He, Him). The central thread that runs through popular evangelicalism (personal spiritual advancement) is the same one that Luther tugged on in the Reformation. In one way or another, our descriptions of Christianity come back around to us. Even if we happen to get the answer correct (God), the constant messaging within our churches is almost always the opposite (us). In the end, our Christian practice is filled with a complexity that is not unlike the complexity Luther faced. If the modern evangelical version of Christianity lacks any one element, it is simplicity. It has always been the simplicity of biblical Christianity that set it against every other religion. There is no other message like this. Faith is an extraordinarily modest means of redemption. "Faith alone" always lands as a radical notion within any system where nothing is ever quite "alone."

As far as the secular world is concerned, the message of Christianity *is* a program of progressive acceptability (moralism). It hardly can be denied from an outsider's perspective that Christians are those people who consider themselves morally superior. Church is where good people go to get away from the bad. There are several notable issues with this perception. First: Christianity is not the only worldview that holds virtue in high regard. Whether religious or otherwise, there are plenty of movements and cultures that produce moral and virtuous people. Second: Christians are constantly betraying this definition of Christianity by their own moral failures. We are people who talk a good game but can't really back it up. Due to our belligerent moralizing, our failures come off with a more spectacular type of hypocrisy than others. Third: Our message is not morality. Our message is "Christ and Him crucified," not man and him improved. While our faith cannot result in anything less than morality, its substance must always be much more. This is primarily because no matter how improved a person may become, morality cannot save an inherently sinful being from the holiness of his Creator. The inability of man to save himself through himself (moralism) is exactly why the Cross was necessary. In a certain way, a Christianity that places the main emphasis on the moral progress of its adherents is an insult to the Cross of Christ (Galatians 2:21). Somewhere along the way, over centuries, a regression has taken place. Certain things that were dismantled have been rebuilt, albeit in a different architecture. Certain things that were liberated at the time of the Reformation have been handed back little by little with the passing of time. We have made a very large U-turn and headed back a previous direction. This is the reason our Christian experience feels like a weight added rather than a burden removed.

The Burden That Remains

The first book I read as a Christian was penned in a prison cell. It was also the first book I ever read cover to cover. Regeneration and love of reading combined for me. I was drawn to *The Pilgrim's*

Progress partly because it was authored by a convict (edgy) and was an allegory (easy). My hope was that the combination would be exciting and interesting, so I set out to read it. Then I put it down. I bought the modern-English version and started over, and then it was both exciting and interesting. The allegorical nature stood out to me because of what the author, John Bunyan, was undertaking—the censure of the very forces that had incarcerated him in the first place. If done well, allegory allows you to stay alive and double down on your convictions at the same time. "Burdens" and "sloughs" have a way of shielding meaning while simultaneously telling the truth. In the case of *Progress*, the brilliance of the literary device almost overshadows the content. It was a stroke of genius. Deniable plausibility.

In 1677, one hundred and fifty-six years after Luther's revolution, Bunyan completed the first part of *The Pilgrim's Progress* within the British prison at Bedfordshire. Altogether, Bunyan served two stints in Bedfordshire—over a twelve-year period—for being a non-conformist. Bunyan, along with other clergy, considered the Church to be spiritually corrupted, therefore, he refused to submit to the authority of the Church of England or to follow the *Book of Common Prayer*. Hence, a "non-conformist." In some ways, *The Pilgrim's Progress* is as much political in its delivery as it is Christian in content—an impressive work of spiritual espionage. Given the union of church and state, the English King, Charles II, had all non-conformists imprisoned for fear they would incite a rebellion against his rule. *The Pilgrim's Progress* was an encrypted sermon delivered to the common people, the very group Bunyan was imprisoned for preaching to in the first place. Bunyan kept preaching despite being jailed, albeit through the image of a rather burdensome backpack.

The Pilgrim's Progress has never gone out of print. By some estimates it is second only to the *Bible* in all-time sales. Undoubtedly, it is the most famous allegory in history. The full title is *The Pilgrim's Progress From This World to That Which Is to Come*. Inspired by his captivity, Bunyan wanted to capture every step in the journey between here and eternity. The journey of the main character, *Christian*, is meant to depict our pilgrimage as believers from this present, temporal state to the eternal one. It's a story about a journey that is the journey we all are on. Through it, Bunyan has instructed countless pilgrims on the progress of the Christian life. The story begins with a man bearing an unbearable burden. Actually, the story begins with a man having a dream about a man bearing an unbearable burden. The man in the dream is *Christian*. But, in reality, he is all of us—the weary human being. The burdened *us*. Christian's awareness of his sin and sense of deserved judgment is crushing. His burden is our "burden." It is the one we all feel whether we acknowledge it or not. Overwhelmed with fear and despair, he leaves his wife and children and sets off to find relief. He's looking for the same thing every human being is looking for—*absolution*. Not long after his departure, Christian comes across a man in a field who knows the exact location of relief.

Then said Evangelist, "Do you see yonder wicket-gate?" The man said, "No." Then said the other, "Do you see yonder shining Light?" He said, "I think I do." Then said Evangelist, "Keep that light in your eye, and go up directly thereto; so shalt thou see the gate; at which, when thou knockest, it shall be told thee what thou shalt do."

These then are the coordinates of Calvary. After a few false starts, challenges, and spiritual quagmires, Christian finally reaches the initial destination of his journey—*mercy*. This moment is the high point of the entire story. I remember the first time I read the scene beneath the cross when the burden was finally removed.

Up this way therefore did burdened Christian run, but not without great difficulty, because of the load on his back. He ran thus till he came at a place somewhat ascending, and upon that place stood a cross, and a little below in the bottom, a sepulchre. So I saw in my dream, that just as Christian came up with the cross, his burden loosed from off his shoulders, and fell from off his back, and began to tumble, and so continued to do, till it came to the mouth of the sepulchre, where it fell in, and I saw it no more.

"It fell in, and I saw it no more." Bunyan profoundly captures the sensation of forgiveness: *weightlessness*. No doubt this is the most eloquent and doctrinal passage in all of Christian fiction (apologies to Lewis fans). I have always appreciated the fact that Bunyan made the pilgrim stand there a while in bewilderment beneath the foolishness of the Cross. It would do the Church good to linger here a while longer than we typically do. Imputation, in all of its mystery, captivates the forgiven.

Over the years I have returned numerous times to these images of grace and forgiveness. All these years later, however, despite its artistry and popularity, I've also come to spot a flaw in Bunyan's classic, a few, actually. I know this might be viewed as sacrilege by many, but I am not the first to note inconsistencies. Some things don't exactly square. I offer these observations with all due respect to Bunyan. I've never been imprisoned for my commitment to the Gospel. Most likely, I never will. I also admit I'm parsing an allegory that, by nature, can be rather broad in meaning. Bunyan does offer a lengthy explanation for his preferred genre. He also penned an unapologetic and encouraging treatise on the Law and Gospel distinction. So we know his commitment to reformed categories. Nonetheless, stop and think about some things for a moment.

Technically speaking, no one pilgrimages to (or for) justification. Justification is not a journey or a path that we must traverse with all sorts of dangers along the way. Neither is there a more determined sort of person who gets there before others. Much seems to depend on the quality rather than the object of Christian's faith. This is not a Protestant notion.

Why do you say that you are righteous only by faith? Not that I am acceptable to God on account of the worthiness of my faith, for only the satisfaction, righteousness, and holiness of Christ is my righteousness before God. I can receive this righteousness and make it mine my own by faith only.

The righteousness offered in the Gospel, and the forgiveness granted in the Cross, are not something we go and get. They are received by faith in a moment upon the effectual call of God. Forgiveness is not an expedition you set out on. Justification is instantaneous. It's punctiliar and not linear. It is by faith and not by works. Absolution is not something for which we have to fight, struggle, and take hold of by resolve, as depicted in the first movement of the story. Evangelist should not have told him where to "go" or what to "do," but in whom to "believe." This part is backward as compared to the actual plot line of the Gospel. Our experience is in the reverse order. Our guilt is removed, and then our journey begins.

Furthermore, the lingering doubt as to whether Christian will finally arrive at the Celestial City casts a shadow over the whole of the story. The conclusion of the journey is characterized more by uncertainty than it is by certainty. The final destination depends more on whether Christian can muster the determination necessary to make it, than it is by God's faithfulness to deliver him.

There is the real suggestion, at numerous points, that Christian could—at any moment—reverse his course, or turn aside, and fall into the very destruction from which he was once delivered. Fundamentally, his arrival in eternity is conditioned on his faithfulness *to* God and not his faith *in* God. Of course, we know that no such uncertainty exists within the promises of the Gospel. Both the end and beginning of the journey are by grace, and one is as certain as the other. We also know that our perseverance depends upon the faithfulness of God to keep His promises to us and not ours to Him. He delivers us. We do not deliver ourselves. Inevitably, we will face our fair share of trials along the way—the greatest of these being our own weakness. But none of these can ever forestall or interrupt our progress toward our final rest. It is as certain as the promises of God are.

> *Who shall separate us from the love of Christ? Shall tribulation, or distress, or persecution, or famine, or nakedness, or danger, or sword? As it is written, "For your sake we are being killed all the day long; we are regarded as sheep to be slaughtered." No, in all these things we are more than conquerors through him who loved us. For I am sure that neither death nor life, nor angels nor rulers, nor things present nor things to come, nor powers, nor height nor depth, nor anything else in all creation, will be able to separate us from the love of God in Christ Jesus our Lord* (Romans 8:35-39).

Finally, not all of our burdens have fallen away. As brilliant as Bunyan's scene at Calvary is, you might get the impression that the load we bear has vanished, never to be seen again. But there is still a weight to bear on the journey *"from this world to that which is to come."* This particular observation is central to the greater point of this book. There is a burden that Bunyan failed to emphasize and make particular. It is the one we are left to bear after our initial burden is removed. It's the one the whole creation feels.

> *For the creation waits with eager longing for the revealing of the sons of God. For the creation was subjected to futility, not willingly, but because of him who subjected it, in hope that the creation itself will be set free from its bondage to corruption and obtain the freedom of the glory of the children of God. For we know that the whole creation has been groaning together in the pains of childbirth until now. And not only the creation, but we ourselves, who have the firstfruits of the Spirit, groan inwardly as we wait eagerly for adoption as sons, the redemption of our bodies. For in this hope we were saved. Now hope that is seen is not hope. For who hopes for what he sees?* (Romans 8:19-24)

For certain, our actual guilt before God, like Christian's, is removed by faith in Christ. His life for ours. The penalty paid. We are free. But the entire burden of sin is not gone, nor is the persistent sense of guilt emanating from the Law of God against our fallen nature. As long as our corruption remains, our feeling of unworthiness goes hand in hand with the simultaneous awareness of our unconditional acceptance.

This conundrum is the fundamental tension of the Christian life. No other religion possesses this tension because no other religion suggests that we are two things at once—saint and sinner. Our wretchedness as fallen human beings is still here. Our lingering sense of unworthiness haunts us. Our deep regret over our corruption lurches up in our hearts causing despair and doubt. There is a burden that will not be removed until we reach our final destination. It is here that the weakness of evangelicalism's message becomes obvious. A religion designed for ongoing improvement cannot possibly grant relief to that conscience dripping with the pangs of its unworthiness and doubt. By its very nature, a message of "how to be better" lacks the mercy necessary to comfort the souls bearing the burden of remaining sin and the reality they will never be perfect in this life.

The "Problem" With *Sola Fide*

The doctrine of *sola fide* is both brilliant and problematic. It is brilliant in that through it God remains both "just and the justifier" in the redemption of sinners. It is problematic in that it creates conflicts exclusive to the Protestant understanding of salvation. The moralistic systems offered by other religions don't possess these same issues. This is often why people prefer mechanical religions (sacerdotal) over those depending exclusively on faith. "Faith alone" is disturbing to many. Roman Catholics refer to salvation within Protestantism as a "hypothetical justification" as compared to the material justification found within their system. We depend on a legal declaration that cannot be held or measured, while theirs is tangible and real.

The most consistent issue created by *sola fide* is the relationship of justification to sanctification. During the Reformation the proper distinction and order of these events was set in place. Sanctification results from and follows justification. Sanctification is not the cause of justification, nor is it simultaneous with it. In some ways the Reformation was a disagreement over how these realities fit together in salvation. Catholicism depended on their being blended together. Protestantism depends on their distinction. Needless to say there are numerous challenges that naturally arise whenever the salvation of sinners is exclusively the work of God through faith. But, these dilemmas are part of who we are.

> *How are you righteous before God? Only by true faith in Jesus Christ.* **Although my conscience accuses me that I have grievously sinned against all God's commandments, have never kept any of them, and am still inclined to all evil, yet God, without any merit of my own, out of mere grace, imputed to me the perfect satisfaction, righteousness, and**

holiness of Christ. He grants these to me as if I had never had nor committed any sin, and as if I myself had accomplished all the obedience which Christ has rendered for me, if only I accept this gift with a believing heart.

Without a doubt, the most personal of these tensions, the one we feel the most, the one we cannot escape in our experience, comes from *simul justus et peccator*—"saint and sinner at the same time." Again, no tension is greater than the one resulting from our being two things at once, both unrighteous and righteous. Under the Protestant schema, the salvation of sinners depends on this seemingly contradictory reality. There is no justification *by faith* if I am a sinner *becoming* a saint. It is part of the mystery resulting from salvation by faith. We are constantly dealing with the internal conflict created by this dilemma. It is never quite still and quiet. It is the Gospel that calms it down. If we aren't constantly managing this struggle we do not rightly understand a reformed view of justification. This tension is the bane of our existence.

We're all constantly compensating for this the unique tension created by *sola fide* in one of two ways. The balancing act is involuntary. First, there is the *sin-versus-progress* approach. This is basic evangelicalism in all of its numerous forms. In this construct you *keep moving*. The struggle here says, "I am not yet *where* I should be." Your aim is to work for, or toward acceptance.

Peace of mind depends on progress. It's what I call the cycle of "progressive acceptability." This view looks inward. The conflict arising in our conscience from our fallen flesh is resolved through ongoing and progressive change. This is where most people live. As we get better we have hope. Faith is in the individual's *ability*. Assurance is a *pursuit*.

Second, there is the *burden-versus-rest* approach. This exists within a traditionally Reformed and confessional perspective. In this construct the struggle is the opposite of the first. We struggle not to keep moving, but to keep resting, trusting, and believing. Therefore, our real challenge is resting in the acceptance of our Heavenly Father *as we* constantly confront the fallout of our sinful condition. In this construct *being still* is the greater challenge. Our guilty flesh will always compel us to work for the acceptance we already possess by faith. What I call the "phantom pain" of condemnation. The struggle here says, "I am by faith *what I know I am not in nature.*" Here the matter is resolved by faith in the promises of God and not by our personal progress. We trust that we are His beloved children although we feel like objects of His disdain. Vivification and mortification take place under the banner of peace with God. This view looks out to Christ. It is more purely a Protestant formation of the Christian life since the tension is resolved by the same reality that created the tension in the first place, *faith*. We are called to rest in God's acceptance through Christ; we are not called to become acceptable.

Augustine's *Incurvatus In Se*

One of the bold assertions of the Christian faith, if not the boldest, is that all men of all ages suffer one basic experience— the awareness of their individual guilt before the God of the Bible. Christianity claims to know at one-and-the-same time what is really wrong with every single member of the human race. We also claim that all men know it themselves but deny it. The giant elephant in humanity is our ever-impending shame and judgment before God. We are constantly subverting this dreadful knowledge with the same sort of annoying vigilance required to hold an inflated ball beneath water. By nature, our guilt is always forcing its way to the surface of our conscience. St. Augustine, by whom all western Christian theology has been plumbed, was the first to categorize this inherent struggle of man's conscience. Augustine described the existential experience of sin's effect on humanity as the *incurvatus in se*. Having turned away from God, our souls are now "turned in on themselves." The resulting distortion haunts all sentient creatures as they search for that which was lost in the Fall and can only be found in their Creator. Augustine aptly captured this ghost in our existence when he wrote, "Thou hast made us for thyself, O Lord, and our heart is restless until it finds its rest in thee." From Augustine's time, until that of the Reformation, all theology revolved around a singular question: "How can sinful man be right with a righteous God?" How do we deal with the burden of our guilt? The struggle for absolution is underneath everything that is human and Christian.

St. Augustine originally diagnosed this loop of despair from within his own experience. A life of debauchery combined with an unending search for meaning only led to deeper misery and emptiness. Around AD 397, following his appointment as Bishop of Hippo, Augustine authored what many regard as the first autobiography of western literature. It is a memoir chronicling his long journey into and out of despair. At the time of its release, *The Confessions* caused something of a scandal. Clergy blushed at the Bishop's honest confession of his lifelong struggle with lust and carnality. No clergyman had ever been so transparent concerning his own sin and humanity. (No clergyman has been as transparent since, nor would they dare.) As you might imagine, the book was widely popular among the laity. But, this popularity was not due to salacious details—it is mild by modern comparisons. It appealed to the masses due to its honesty about the human condition. There was hope offered to the common man. If the brilliant bishop was himself a sinner (under the same conditions) who had received unmerited grace, certainly that same grace was available to them. Augustine was the first theologian to offer an honest appraisal of the full effects of sin on fallen man. He said what every man knew but was afraid to admit: *the effects are total.*

Augustine's greatest impact on Christian thought and theology was on the topic of sin. He revolutionized Christian thinking by orienting all theological categories around the concept of original sin. Understanding man to be inherently sinful was a tectonic shift in theological speculation. All men receive in their persons both the guilt and corruption of Adam. As a result, we all are inherently guilty and under the curse of spiritual death before we do anything. It can be easily argued that this single idea is the most significant observation in the history of theological formation. It remains the essential dividing line of all theological systems. While the implications and corollaries are too vast to discuss in this chapter, there are two that are central. First, if man's will is included in the effects of the Fall (his will is bound by sin) then man can never be the effectual cause of his salvation. Second, if man is unable to contribute to his salvation, then salvation must result completely from an act of grace on the part of God. One is the inevitable consequence of the other. Once Augustine fell upon the reality of original sin, grace was inevitable.

Augustine grasped something that had eluded the thinkers who had gone before him: Sin is a *state* before it is an *action*. Sin is a *condition* man is in before it is an *act* he commits. It was the act of disobedience of our federal head that led to the preexistent condition of his posterity. (Correspondingly, it is the obedience of, Christ, which liberates us from the effects of the first man.) There is no way to overstate the significance of this one idea. Augustine's doctrine of original sin essentially eradicated moralism. With no capacity to merit God's favor, man's efforts are useless. With Augustine, there is a real sense in which man must be pitied (state) even before he is accused (act). We do what we do because of who we are. We are who we are because of what someone else did. This clarification is devastating and reassuring at the same time. It devastates us because it means we are helpless before a holy God. It encourages us because it leads us to the message of God's grace found in the Gospel. Whenever the proper sequence of these realities (condition then action) has been misplaced, the inevitable outcome is always "progressive acceptability."

Evangelicalism completely misses Augustine's distinction. The idea of sin as a state is lost on us. We have been conditioned to view sin primarily, if not singularly, in behavioral and moral categories. This is pietism's centuries-old effect on the Church. Sin has become primarily about behavior. This is where the ever-present thread of self-improvement within evangelicalism comes from. But in reality, at the base of Christianity, sin is first and foremost about *being* prior to *doing*. The Gospel corresponds exactly to this emphasis. The core of the Gospel offers a change in identity prior to and leading to a change in action. This is why the message of the modern church (spiritual improvement) tends to add to the burden of the weary pilgrim rather than lighten it.

When the proper sequence (state prior to act) is reversed, or goes missing in the Church, everything is flipped. When it is in proper order, things change dramatically. For example, when we understand sin as a state, the ordinary means at the saint's disposal exist mainly to comfort the anxious soul. It is a declaration of the promises of God toward our burdened soul. Through the Word, prayer, and the sacrament of the Lord's Table we are strengthened in our trust in Christ. Our faith is established in Christ and our confidence in God's grace towards us increases. Through these ordinary means, the weary heart feeds on the assurance of God's benevolence towards it. By these simple measures, we rest in Christ even as we battle on.

When we understand sin exclusively in behavioral categories, the means at our disposal become an end in themselves. The goal is self-improvement rather than (or over and above) trust in God's promise. The Bible is approached as a handbook for spirituality rather than a historic record of God's unending faithfulness. Prayer becomes a method of spiritual centering rather than a way for the exhausted child to call out to the Father. The sacrament of the Lord's Table becomes a moment we come to double down on our commitment to God, rather than resting in His commitment to us.

The earliest of our reformed confessions made the appropriate distinction between state and action. They read very differently than our literature reads. They are a call to lean exclusively on Christ. They speak of the Gospel within the framework of our collective misery, the dread that befalls us, and the singular remedy found in God's free grace. The *Belgic Confession* describes our justification as the means by which our "fear, dread and terror of God's approach" is relieved. The *Heidelberg Catechism* opens with questions concerning the reality of our "misery" and the source of our "comfort." The *Westminster Larger Catechism* admits the "continual and irreconcilable war" which takes place in our Christian experience. These documents approach our sin as a state from which we have been freed and are being delivered. As a result, what you find in the reformers—and the reformed confessions—that you don't find in modern evangelicalism, is sympathy for our weakness and shared condition.

Our Christianity has been retrofitted with the American ethos that has no place for the weak or weakness. Our incessant messaging of self-improvement and progress drowns the offering of assurances found in the Gospel. When you read the works of Augustine, Luther, or Calvin you find a very different tone from the one coming from evangelicalism. Their works are saturated with a deep sympathy for the beleaguered. What's critical to observe is how the first generation reformers (along with Augustine) saw it as their duty to run beside the life of the pilgrim and offer a message of hope in their weariness. They held out compassion rather than pointing to goals. Their first concern was not that we be constantly improving, but that we be constantly believing. They persistently pointed out the uselessness of moralism in redemption. We have confused the two.

Luther's *Anfechtung*

Luther was well acquainted with the misery and subterranean distress of the human condition. He called it his *anfechtung*— "terror of the soul." His early religious life was devoted to relieving the pain of his own conscience and the primal realization of his helplessness and guilt before his Creator. Luther has often been referred to as the "pioneer" of the human conscience in that he set out to finally answer our lingering question. In reality, Luther merely uncovered the tracks that Augustine left in seeking out the same answer. But, ultimately, both Augustine and Luther traced the steps of the Apostle Paul who had already undertaken this quest. Paul's answer had lain for centuries under the moralism of the Dark Ages by the time Luther found it. *Man is saved by grace alone.* He is redeemed in the same sequence in which he fell: position to condition. In the sin of Adam, man lost his position of innocence, and the corruption of his flesh immediately followed. In Christ, by faith, our status is restored (justification), our disposition begins its realignment (sanctification), and our temporal existence will finally end in our rescue from this fallen realm (glorification). We are saved, and we are being saved. We exist in a *both/and* dimension. As was previously mentioned, this duality is central to a reformed faith. We are saints (status), but we are also sinners (nature). Justification was not a process. It was this particular truth that sparked the "Copernican Revolution" of sixteenth-century Christianity, commonly referred to as the Protestant Reformation. Before this moment, there was no *both/and*, there was only *either/or*. Either you are a saint (righteous), or you are a sinner (unrighteous). In this paradigm, salvation could only ever be the process of moving from one to the other. The Church offered the means of becoming accceptable before God, but it could never offer any assurance this would actually happen.

Herein lies the great dilemma of redemption. How can God be just and forgive sinners He must condemn? How can man be sinful and yet be just before God? It is this contradiction that trapped Luther in an unending loop of despair. No matter how diligently he employed the means offered to him by the Church, he could not find rest. Luther's fiercest critics have suggested his real problem did not lie with the Church but with his hyperactive conscience. Essentially, Luther worried too much. The Roman Church was not wrong; Luther needed Xanax. But, truth be known, Luther saw things as they actually are. Namely, rest is impossible in a scheme where all depends on unending effort toward an unreachable goal. He was right to worry. Luther was himself a pilgrim who entered into the Church to unload his burden only to find a greater weight. In the end, he worked the system to its logical conclusion—*futility*. It was here, at the end of hope, where hope finally came rushing in. His breakthrough moment has been referenced by Protestants constantly since it occurred, but, his "tower experience" bears repeating here, given the current discussion.

> *I meditated night and day on those words until at last, by the mercy of God, I paid attention to their context: "The justice of God is revealed in it, as it is written: 'The just person lives by faith.'" I began to understand that in this verse the justice of God is*

*that by which the just person lives by a gift of God,
that is by faith. I began to understand that this verse
means that the justice of God is revealed through the
Gospel, but it is a passive justice, i.e. that by which
the merciful God justifies us by faith, as it is written:
"The just person lives by faith."*

In his cloister Luther came to the despairing realization that moral improvement was completely inadequate to justify men before God, or to salve their consciences. Assurance that originates in our relative morality is no assurance at all. What Luther finally despaired of was his sinful self. He came to understand that the salvation he sought must come to him from outside; it must be provided by another as a gift. It must be an act of pure grace. It must be received by faith. Once this dawned in Luther's heart, he immediately realized the fundamental struggle of the Christian life was one of faith.

For Luther, *anfechtung* was a lifelong condition the redeemed cannot outrun. The struggle is permanent this side of eternity. As he once wrote, "Here is the paradox at the heart of the Christian self-perception: A godly man feels sin more than grace, wrath more than favor, judgment more than redemption." Therefore, resting in what God has accomplished by his Son is a permanent feature of our experience and not a one-time deal. All of our life is lived beneath the sky of His justifying grace as we journey along a path of doubt, hardship, and pain. This perspective was the origin of Luther's theology of the Cross. Within the triumphalism of evangelicalism (victorious Christian life) suffering is viewed more as an abnormality. The Gospel is always behind us. Within a reformed world, suffering is the norm and the Gospel hovers over us declaring God's goodness in the midst of pain. When Luther famously commented, "experience alone makes a theologian" he was speaking of the experience of pain. Near the end of his life Luther wrote, "If I should live a little while longer, I would like to write a book about *Anfechtung*. Without it no man can rightly understand the Holy Scriptures or know what the fear and love of God is all about. In fact, without *Anfechtung* one does not really know what the spiritual life is."

The only cure for our inevitable despair is a constant announcement to the contrary. The most primitive struggle of the Christian pilgrimage—even before the mortification of the flesh—is faith. The battle is trusting that God is good with us in Christ when everything in us doubts it. We may be called children of God from above but feel like His enemies on the ground of our experience. In one sense, the Christian is no different than any other man. "God justifies the ungodly." He is a human sinner (saved by grace) who still bears the burden of his fallen condition. But there is also a very real difference between the Christian and his neighbor. One significant difference lies in the source of the Christian's hope. By faith he has placed any assurance of his acceptance before God in the promises found in the Gospel of His grace. Even though we have received the righteousness of Christ by faith as a covering, we still live and exist within the rubble of destruction caused by Adam. As the Law of God reigns down upon our conscience, the Gospel of God's good favor calms our souls with news of mercy and peace. Luther saw his task as a pastor to be inundating the weary pilgrim with reminders of good news, rather than driving him from behind with threats and doubt.

In all of church history, there is no figure who so vehemently defended the saint against any thing or person that might distract him from faith in Christ. The fury that he leveled against his moralizing adversaries is legendary. The biting sarcasm and unrelenting insults in his exchange with Erasmus in *On the Bondage of the Will* are a prime example. His arguments are logically devastating and wrapped in one personal slight after another. But underneath this intensity was a determination to protect the common man from the error of the Church that had so long locked him in darkness. When you read Luther's works, you cannot help but sense his concern for our faith. You feel as if he is writing for you personally. He was most effective when he was diagnosing the fear that befalls our hearts, and chasing it from us with proclamations of God's good favor. He knew that relief came not by fleeing to monasteries but by fleeing to Christ.

> *We are born in sin. To doubt the good will of God is an inborn suspicion of God with all of us. Besides, the devil, our adversary, goeth about seeking to devour us by roaring: "God is angry at you and is going to*

*destroy you forever." In all these difficulties we have
only one support, the Gospel of Christ. To hold on to
it, that is the trick. Christ cannot be perceived with
the senses. We cannot see Him. The heart does not feel
His helpful presence. Especially in times of trials a
Christian feels the power of sin, the infirmity of his
flesh, the goading darts of the devil, the agues of death,
the scowl and judgment of God. All these things cry
out against us. The Law scolds us, sin screams at us,
death thunders at us, the devil roars at us. In the
midst of the clamor the Spirit of Christ cries in our
hearts: "Abba, Father." And this little cry of the Spirit
transcends the hullabaloo of the Law, sin, death, and
the devil, and finds a hearing with God.*

Calvin's Assurance as the Essence

When we think about John Calvin, what typically comes to
mind is *Institutes of the Christian Religion*. When we think about
Institutes of the Christian Religion, we're usually overwhelmed.
It's one of the more lofty books in all of Christian literature,
coming from one of the more intimidating theological minds in
the history of the Church. For most people, Calvin's thoughts
represent an inaccessible body of work so cerebral and advanced
it has no real application to everyday life. It was a scholastic
work written to the intellectual elite of his day. But this is where
we have it wrong with Calvin. Holed up somewhere outside of

Paris, running for his life from Catholic authorities, Calvin wrote *Institutes* in defense of the French peasant and commoner. It is an introduction to the Christian faith and was intended to be an elementary understanding of the Reformed faith. Calvin calls its contents "rudiments" of understanding. He describes the aim of *Institutes* in the introduction:

> *And I undertook this labor especially for our French countrymen, very many of whom I knew to be hungering and thirsting for Christ; but I saw very few who had been imbued with the slightest knowledge of him. The book itself witnesses that this was my intention, adapted as it is to a simple and, you may say, elementary form of teaching.*

You have to laugh at Calvin's description. "Simple" and "elementary" are not the characteristics that typically come to mind. "Advanced" and "difficult" are closer to how people feel when they consider opening its pages. This is why most people who would identify as "Calvinists" have never read it. But Calvin wrote his *Institutes* as a way to preserve the simplicity of the Gospel against the codification of the Church. He saw it as his duty to defend the unadorned faith of his fellow Frenchmen against scholasticism, political intimidation, and the threat of death. Calvin stood between that hostility and the humble flock of believers who had trusted in Christ alone. Despite the characterizations that have come down to us through history, his

Institutes is as compassionate and pastoral a work as has ever been authored.

Calvin was a pastor before he was a scholar. He cared deeply about the burden that Christians carry in their temporal state, and how it distresses their faith. He also observed how the Church had robbed the saint of assurance by creating a "labyrinth" of doubt. This is why, in his *magnum opus*, you will find both a heart overflowing with kindness on the one hand, and a scorching rebuke against moralists on the other. If *Institutes* are to be understood rightly, they must be seen as one man's effort at guarding the simple faith for simple people. This feature is borne out in numerous places throughout *Institutes*, but no section more so than book three chapter two. His reflections on faith and assurance are profound and life altering. They are all intended to drive the believer's faith into the bedrock of God's grace. It is here that Calvin famously defines assurance as the essence of the Christian life:

> *Now we shall possess a right definition of faith if we call it a firm and certain knowledge of God's benevolence towards us, founded upon the truth of the freely given promise in Christ, both revealed in our minds and sealed upon our hearts through the Holy Spirit.*

Assurance is what the Gospel provides. As he wrote, "*Now it is an assurance that renders the conscience calm and peaceful before God's judgment.*" (*Institutes* III, II, 16) We will not always have a perfect sense of assurance in this life, but by faith in Christ we possess absolute assurance of our future acceptance before God. It matters not what our sense of it might be at any moment. True assurance rests solely in the faithfulness of God. It is not the quality of our faith, but the object of it, that saves and sustains us. Like Luther, Calvin observed the tension that would characterize our lives as Christians:

> *Therefore, the godly heart feels in itself a division because it is partly imbued with sweetness from its recognition of divine goodness, partly grieves in bitterness from an awareness of its calamity; partly rests upon the promise of the Gospel, partly trembles at the evidence of its own iniquity, partly rejoices in at the expectation of life, partly shudders at death. This variation arises from the imperfection of faith, since in the course of the present life it never goes so well with us that we are wholly cured of the disease of unbelief and entirely possessed by faith. Hence arise those conflicts; when unbelief, which reposes in the remains of the flesh, rises up to attack the faith that has been inwardly conceived.*

It was Calvin who finally pulled the deadly mixture of faith and faithfulness apart after centuries had tangled them together in an impossible knot. Calvin sought to distinguish the faithfulness of God from our faithfulness to Him. Assurance lies not in our faithfulness as Christians, but in His faithfulness to us. It is our faith in His faithfulness that sustains us, and not our faithfulness to Him—the object of faith and not the quality of it. It is not hard to imagine that if Calvin were writing with the same purpose in our day, he would be taking up arms against us. We do more to pull the two realities back together and erode the confidence of the saints than we imagine. What's important to note in Calvin is that assurance is the essence of the Christian life and not the pursuit of it. Meaning that true faith in Christ is to possess the assurance that we shall be accepted by God. Underneath the burden of our corruption we will inevitably be weighed down with doubt and misery. It is here that faith lifts our heads up to behold the good news delivered in the Gospel. God is good with us, not due to anything in us, but due to the mystery of His grace. Dear saint, He will indeed receive you. So certain is our future, we face judgment with an absolute confidence in Christ to deliver us. Calvin's thoughts here are unbelievably encouraging to the weary soul.

> *Hence arises a wonderful consolation: that we perceive judgment to be in the hands of him who has already destined us to share with him the honor of judging (cf. Matt. 19:28)! Far indeed is he from mounting his judgment seat to condemn us! How could our most merciful Ruler destroy his people?*

How could the Head scatter his own members? How could our Advocate condemn his clients? For if the apostle dares exclaim that with Christ interceding for us there is no one who can come forth to condemn us (Rom. 8:34, 33), it is much more true, then, that Christ as Intercessor will not condemn those whom he has received into his charge and protection. No mean assurance, this—that we shall be brought before no other judgment seat than that of our Redeemer, to whom we must look for our salvation! Moreover, he who now promises eternal blessedness through the gospel will then fulfill his promise in judgment. Therefore, by giving all judgment to the Son (John 5:22), the Father has honored him to the end that he may care for the consciences of his people, who tremble in dread of judgment.

Paul's Already Not Yet

When the epistle to the Romans opens, it opens on mankind trapped in a doomed and warped creation. We find humanity held captive by sin. Mankind is pictured with the ear of its soul up against the wall of eternity listening to the muffled existence of their Creator on the other side. We know He is there, and that we belong to Him, but we are unable to traverse the divide of existences. In truth, we have no real idea of what life originally felt like. All that is an echo now. Having attempted to rob the

Lord of His glory, we locked ourselves into the vault of our own condemnation. Having assumed that we would be set free from God by our self-will, we imprisoned ourselves, as recounted in Romans 1:24-25. Romans 1 is not a description of the worst people we can imagine, nor is it a description of how bad things can get. It's a description of *who* we presently are; living under the constant delusion of sin's effect.

Paul depicts sin as a force; it is a "law" that is all around us and constantly distorting our perspective. We have no idea what it means to be without sin. Sin is the constant—almost imperceptible—struggle we have felt since we were first self-conscious. It is all we have ever known. Whatever "sinless" meant for Adam, we've no sense of it at all. Sin is a blindness. We live in squalor and perceive it as a palace. Not surprisingly, with Paul sin is more than an act we commit against God. It is an existence that separates us from God. An atmosphere. A virus that has been downloaded into every layer of our life. It is a worldwide insanity. It surrounds us all the time. It is in how we see things. It is in how we think of God. It is in how we perceive each other. It is in how we feel things. It is in how we desire things. It is in what we desire, and that we desire the wrong things. It is in our fears. It is in our emotions. It is the root of all our insecurities, angers, lusts, deceptions, excuses, and conflicts. It is all we know. It is bondage.

As Paul begins Romans 6, he has returned to this opening image of man's doom. When Paul describes sin in this chapter, he describes it as a power, or a controlling force—a sphere from which we cannot deliver ourselves. When we were born, we were born into this dominion. The apostle personifies sin as a tyrant ruling over the broken dominion of the first Adam. We are enslaved to sin (Romans 6:7). It has dominion over us (Romans 6:9,14). It reigns over our existence (Romans 6:12). We are its slaves (Romans 6:17). We are subject to the triangulation of sin's guilt, death's torment, and the law's condemnation. The image of a dark and despotic domain dominates the chapter. This is because he wants us to view our salvation as a divine transfer from one domain to the other. Paul borrows from the language of captivity and the exodus to describe our condition and deliverance. In essence, Romans 6 is a description of our rescue from the domain and rule of sin under the first Adam to that of the final Adam, Christ.

This helps us understand what Paul means by his central question, "How can we who died to sin still live in it?" Clearly, he is presenting sin as a state and condition. Paul does not tell us to stop committing sinful acts, but that we no longer have to. He does not say, "How can we who died to sin continue to sin?" He asks essentially, "Why would we who died to it be subject to it anymore?" The idea itself is simple. When you die, the laws of your existence and ruling authorities no longer have authority over you. You are freed from that domain. If I die in prison, the warden may shout orders at me, but I am not obligated to respond. When I die I am no longer subject to my previous existence. The bills may pile up in my mailbox, but I'm not going to pay them. I'm dead.

If I die to sin's domain, I don't have to pay sin's bill or answer the door when its deception comes calling. In Christ, you died to sin's domain and were raised within a new domain with a new status.

Evangelicalism has largely understood this chapter as a description of the inner workings of sanctification, or the process of transformation. We take it to mean, "Here's how you stop sinning." But in reality the message is: "Here's why you no longer have to sin." Paul wants us to understand how the change in our status changes our perception of life. We live from our position in Christ forward. Sanctification is more about not having to do what we did before and less about avoiding bad things we once did. Evangelical definitions of transformation sound like a new sort of bondage. Sanctification sounds like a trip to the dentist. But, sanctification is about the freedom we now have to live as we should. Paul never offers sanctification as the measuring stick of God's pleasure toward us. Rather, sanctification results from His grace toward us. Sanctification is an eye-opening awareness to the deception of sin and the joy of obedience in Christ. Sanctification is coming to see life in a completely different way. It is not our ongoing efforts at staying out of trouble. It is an invitation to freedom. Whatever sanctification includes, it begins with an understanding of who we are in Christ and what He has freed us from.

It is remarkably clear that Paul understood the battle lines of our life to be drawn down the middle of two statuses: who we once were in Adam, and who we are now in Christ. Paul grasps the tension that our new existence creates. We live in an in-between place where our position in Christ has not yet terminated in our full possession of Christ. While we are not legally subject to the laws of this fallen domain, we are, nonetheless, on a pilgrimage through it. Sin will try to assume its previous authority. Death will still shout its threats. The Law will assail our burdened consciences. He goes on to perfectly capture the frustration of our "already not yet" status. How we, on occasion, get pulled into a previous existence.

> *For I delight in the law of God, in my inner being, but I see in my members another law waging war against the law of my mind and making me captive to the law of sin that dwells in my members. Wretched man that I am! Who will deliver me from this body of death?* (Romans 7:22-24)

Paul answers his own question in the next verse: *Thanks be to God through Jesus Christ our Lord!* Paul got it. He understood that the on-the-ground, day-to-day battle is remembering who we are in Christ. This, of course, leads to living within the sphere of Christ. Again, the battle is believing. It is battling while we believe. Because of our remaining corruption, we will fail. Because of our failures, we will doubt. What we require in this moment is an assurance of God's benevolence. Only the Gospel of Christ can provide this. This is what Paul does in Romans 8:1-4:

> *There is therefore now no condemnation for those*
> *who are in Christ Jesus. For the law of the Spirit*
> *of life has set you free in Christ Jesus from the law*
> *of sin and death. For God has done what the law,*
> *weakened by the flesh, could not do. By sending his*
> *own Son in the likeness of sinful flesh and for sin, he*
> *condemned sin in the flesh, in order that the righteous*
> *requirement of the law might be fulfilled in us, who*
> *walk not according to the flesh but according to the*
> *Spirit.*

Despite all evidence to the contrary, there is no reason to fear. He remains our Father.

> *For you did not receive the spirit of slavery to fall*
> *back into fear, but you have received the Spirit of*
> *adoption as sons, by whom we cry, "Abba! Father!"*
> *The Spirit himself bears witness with our spirit*
> *that we are children of God, and if children, then*
> *heirs—heirs of God and fellow heirs with Christ.*
> (Romans 8:15-17)

CHAPTER FOUR

Finding the "On" Switch

Everyone likes a good "fixer-upper." Or at least my wife and I do. For us it's exciting to look past the dust and grime of a dated item and bring it back to life. It's amazing how a new coat of paint and a little TLC can produce so much dramatic change. Seeing what we can "make of something" keeps us looking for our next project. But we've learned a few things after completing several projects, including: It's impossible to paint one wall. Without fail, the moment you paint one, the imperfections of the others come into view. You have to be ready to paint all the walls if you start messing with even one. This book is like that. We hope by this time you're looking at the one painted wall of confessionalism. But once contrasted with the historic confessional realities of "Vintage Faith," you might be realizing some other blemishes that need to be addressed. Before you walk out of the room, assuming the renovation job is complete, lets take a look at the other "walls." There's more work to be done.

Christians are "people of the book." Our lives in Christ are shaped directly by the pages of Scripture. We affirm the Bible as our only source of divine information and, appropriately, "blame" the Bible for what we do and how we live. The Bible is always present in our Christian education and training. Passages, parables, and proverbs are offered so you can know how to live your life in Christ. I hope you feel comfortable with your Bible; that you can keep up in a good-old-fashioned "sword drill," and that you have memorized select passages. But I need to warn you, your view of the Bible could be confused in more ways than you might imagine.

Undoubtedly at some point, either at a young age or directly after you were converted, someone handed you a Bible and said, "You're going to need this." The Bible is commonly promoted as "the book that will change your life." And that's true. Christians do "need the Bible" and it will "change your life." But maybe not in the way you've been told. A lot is assumed about the Bible. Here's what I mean. I'm sure you've been taught what the Bible *says*—passages of Scripture have been explained, verses have been memorized, applications have been applied. But have you been taught what the Bible is *about*—how all the individual verses and characters relate to the singular message of the Bible? More often than not, the difference between what the Bible *says* and what it is *about* is overlooked. The assumption is that the former is equivalent to the latter. To be fair, knowing what the Bible *says* is definitely part of understanding the singular message of the Bible. But, even if you memorize all of the "important" passages, it's still possible you can miss what the Bible is all *about*.

Recently I saw a YouTube video of a construction worker, one of those "fail videos." A construction worker was standing on a ladder demolishing a concrete wall. The man was holding an electric jackhammer and confidently accomplishing the task at hand. Now instead of using the tool how it was originally designed, this poor soul was wielding it like a hundred-pound chisel. Thrusting it into the wall, he slowly chipped away the unwanted material. The fellow workers who handed him the tool assumed it was self-explanatory. But clearly it was not. Mercifully someone comes along and plugs in the jackhammer and says "OK, now use it." After looking down at his friend the construction work goes right back to "chiseling" away the concrete. Finally, his friend, realizing the tool is not as "self-explanatory" as he thought, stops the man and points to the "on" switch. Instantly the work gets easier. The tool he had been using one way was designed to be used in another. All along he had the very tool needed to make his work easy. Someone just had to tell him how to use it.

Unfortunately, our experience with the Bible is very much like this jackhammer. The Bible is the most assumed tool in the Christian toolbox. It's handed to us early on in our Christian life and assumed we know what to do with it and how to use it.

Sermons are preached from the Bible but rarely do people hear about the purpose of the Bible. I fell victim to this very problem. I knew a lot about the Bible. It had always been a part of my life. I knew numerous details. I could recite all sixty-six books in order. I was familiar with its structure, themes, and content. I even have a piece of paper declaring that I received a degree in the subject of the Bible. But with all that, I still found the Bible difficult to understand and even harder to apply. I just assumed that was how God intended it.

The inability to understand the point of the Bible should come as no great surprise. The majority of believers are never empowered to answer the simple question, "*What* is the point of the Bible?" Our focus is primarily directed toward *how* believers can apply the Bible. Often, it's the easier question to answer. But for so many unsuspecting Christians, focusing predominately on the "*how*" question can, and has, obscured the greater point of the Bible. I understand the Bible is a complex and diverse book. It's made up of numerous characters and a variety of themes. It can be hard to see the common link through it all. How can you ever boil it down to one singular point? The greatest irony is that the people "of the book" struggle to even understand what "the book" is all about.

Truth be told, the Church and evangelicalism haven't made it easy. We meant well. But I believe history will show that we have done a disservice to the Bible. No other time period has produced more material about the Bible while missing it's point entirely. Take a glance at your bookshelf for a moment. It's probably filled with material written over the last fifty years that over-spiritualize and over-complicate the Christian life. There has really only been one type of book written in recent years. Each book takes a specific problem and offers a list of verses than can be applied in order to "fix" the problem. The cover art might be different, but the structure is all the same. It goes something like this: "Consider these two illustrations of biblical characters, memorize this list of verses and your problem will go away." The byproduct of this approach is that we've been trained to view the Bible as a "self-help" book covering thousands of subjects: personal ethics, a rich religious life, steps for personal blessing, ways to deter sin, etc. The actual story of the Bible has become muddled and confusing. Instead of a story written *for* us, it's a story written *about* us. Here's what I mean. It can be surprising to find out that the "improvement of mankind" is not the main focus of the Bible. Obviously, we're a part of the story. But we are not at the center. The particular message of Christianity goes far beyond personal improvement.

Here is another way we have confused the point of the Bible. The Bible has been stripped apart and served up *a la carte*. The individual stories and characters have been unreasonably separated from the greater context. In many cases, the supporting characters have been pulled out and placed in their own books where they become the main character. If publishers or evangelical leaders could make a "sequel" to the Bible by emphasizing the works of a supporting character, they've done it. Often, our Christian culture spends more time figuring out how to repackage the Bible and not enough time trying to understand the Bible. It's sad, but many have been more influenced by the actions of King David over their Christian lives than they have been by the actions of Jesus. As a recent newsmagazine essay pointed out, "The Bible is not the book many American fundamentalists and political opportunists think it is, or more precisely, what they want it to be." That same essay wisely declared, "The good book is so misquoted it's a sin." It's unfortunate, but many have unintentionally robbed the Bible of the story of redemption and replaced it with a story of personal fulfillment.

In what follows, I want to help refocus your attention and, possibly, offer the introductory training lesson you have always needed. Believers need Scripture, but if we don't know how to use it, or why it was given, we're bound to misapply or neglect it altogether.

Where To Begin

You and I have never known a time when Scripture wasn't present. It's been a normal feature of our history. It continues to be the most-sold book in existence. We take for granted that it has always been there. Therefore, we don't naturally question why the Bible was given. It's actually a very helpful exercise. Why did God use forty men, over thousands of years, in three different languages, to explain all the details contained in this book? Why did God spend the time and effort to offer us the information contained within the canon of Scripture? Why give us the Bible? Many faithful Bible-saturated Christians struggle to answer this simple question. Many are stumped when asked, "What is the singular point and purpose of the Bible?" Several popular choices have been promoted. I want to walk through a few of the options and point out some holes that exist. You might discover your go-to answer makes the list below.

Apologetic View: Prove the Existence of God

The first option many hold is this: The Bible was given so we can know that God exists, and glorify Him accordingly. The details contained within primarily carry an apologetic purpose. Those holding to this option approach the Bible as a proof text for everything from the existence of God to the six-day creation of the world. Every problem in life can find its solution in a Bible verse. It might sound counterintuitive, and even unchristian, but we don't need the Bible for everything. Consider the existence of God. One might assume that without the Bible we would have no knowledge of God. But according to Romans 1:20 and the concept of general revelation, it declares that our knowledge of Him is written on the heart. Therefore, the Bible must have been written for something greater than just telling us about God's existence. The knowledge of God was present well before any words of Scripture were written down. The apologetic option falls short.

Theological View: Premillennial Dispensational Leanings

Another option promoted is that everything in the Bible sets up the Kingdom of God. Israel is the chief example of this goal. God, working in the hearts and lives of people and nations, will bring about His kingdom. Because Israel failed to accomplish that goal, the Church was then instituted to complete the task. This view also sees the Church as a parenthesis to God's plan. Israel was the focus; the Church was instituted because Israel failed. Jesus therefore came to establish God's kingdom. There is the issue with this view: Jesus didn't have to die in order to establish His kingdom. The primary question that has to be answered with this view is this: Why did Christ first come as a lamb led to the slaughter and not on a white horse wielding the sword? Clearly, God's kingdom will be established in the end. But this option is insufficient at including everything found in Scripture.

Ethical View: The Bible Was Given To Make Us Better People

This third option is probably the most popular; the Bible was given so we have examples to follow. God offers the men and women contained within as role models. If we are going to live God-honoring lives we should exemplify the attributes of the biblical characters. David has been set up as the model for being a "man after God's own heart." Nehemiah exists to exemplify godly leadership. Esther is our example of true faith. Jabez best demonstrates a faithful prayer life. Moses' "burning bush" is an example of a biblical decision-making moment. While this approach might preach well, how does Christ fit into it all? Do we really need Christ if the purpose of the Bible is to imitate these figures? Of course not! Therefore, the Bible cannot merely be a photo album of men and women of faithfulness. God must have given us the Bible for a greater reason than simply to encourage us to live better lives through imitation.

These methods might seem sufficient. Clearly each can explain portions of Scripture. But overall, they fall short. The failure lies in their inability to explain all of Scripture. With each option, there are portions of the Bible that just don't make sense as to why they were included or excluded. If the purpose of the Bible is for apologetics, why didn't God give a greater defense for six-day creation? Or, if the Kingdom of God is the point, why spend so much time in the Epistles equipping the local church? If ethics is the goal, what should you do with the major and minor prophets? It's difficult to boil everything found in Scripture down to one simple point. There is a lot it has to cover. The point of the Bible must fit into this equation: it must be broad enough to include everything, yet specific enough to define it. The options above failed to accomplish this. Frankly, there is only one option capable of fulfilling this formula. And the way to get to that formula is not by asking *what* Scripture can be used for, which is ultimately what the other options focus upon. The solution to our equation comes by asking, *why* Scripture was the tool God determined to hand us. It's not until you learn and understand the *why* that you can appropriately apply the *what* to your life.

Why Give Us the Book?

The Bible is a multifaceted book with a simple message at the core. From beginning to end, the Bible declares how sinful man can be reconciled to a holy God. Contained within the sixty-six books are numerous details covering a litany of aspects, but the story of redemptive grace is at the center. Theologians call this perspective the "redemptive-historical view of Scripture." This is the reformed understanding that everything in Scripture is connected by one overarching theme—the redemption of sinners. The theme of redemption is central to the message of the Bible. Every book, every person, every event in Scripture is linked to this reality. Some of the connections are clearer than others at first glance, but they all point back to this central reality. "Redemption" is broad enough to include everything found in Scripture, yet specific enough to explain everything. With this theme in mind, you can jump into any portion of Scripture—Old or New Testament, history or prophecy, doctrine or ethics— and explain why it's there. The redemptive-historical view helps us hold everything in context. It describes how the many details fit together to declare one simple message—the gospel of God's grace toward unworthy sinners. The redemptive-historical view is the "on" switch for the Bible. With this view we can use Scripture as God intended.

Because of this central focus of redemption, there is continuity between the various books of the Bible. The Bible will not contradict itself, and therefore, the Old Testament declares the same truth as the New Testament. The Gospel can be clearly seen throughout Scripture. Practically speaking, if your interpretation of a passage contradicts the consistent teaching of Scripture elsewhere, your interpretation, not the rest of Scripture, is wrong. The reformers declared that there is unity and perspicuity (meaning clarity) in Scripture. That's not to say that everything in Scripture is necessarily easy to understand. But, as one writer states, "What we must understand in order to be saved is clear." The *Westminster Confession of Faith*, Chapter 1:7 states,

> *All things in Scripture are not alike plain in themselves, nor alike clear unto all: yet those things which are necessary to be known, believed, and observed for salvation, are so clearly propounded, and opened in some place of Scripture or other, that not only the learned, but the unlearned, in a due use of the ordinary means, may attain unto a sufficient understanding of them.*

The continuity in the redemptive-historical view allows us to keep the greater context in focus while mining the specifics of each passage. Whether you're reading large sections, or intensely dissecting a few short verses, you can confidently do so knowing you will not be led astray from the overarching theme. If I might use the ever-popular tree and forest analogy—we often become so caught up in the nuances of each individual tree that we forget to study the forest. The redemptive-historical view helps to keep in focus the whole forest while better learning the individual trees.

The redemptive-historical view also serves as a safety net every time Scripture is opened. So many pastors assume if they just teach the text on any specific Sunday they will be safe. But there's more going on in the story than what meets the eye. God revealed specific details of redemption in a progressive manner. It takes the overarching view of redemption to fully understand what's going on at any given moment. The apostle Peter spoke of this reality in 1 Peter 1:10-12:

> *Concerning this salvation, the prophets who prophesied about the grace that was to be yours searched and inquired carefully, inquiring what person or time the Spirit of Christ in them was indicating when he predicted the sufferings of Christ and the subsequent glories. It was revealed to them that they were serving not themselves but you, in the things that have now been announced to you through those who preached the good news to you by the Holy Spirit sent from heaven, things into which angels long to look.*

We are blessed to live on this side of Christ. We get to see the whole story from beginning to end. We would be foolish to not consider redemption when determining the details of any given text.

This is Nothing New

Allow me to walk you through some important history for a moment. At the heart of the Reformation was the doctrine of *sola scriptura*—the declaration that Scripture is the ultimate and final authority for the Christian. It's the declaration that started it all. It is safe to assume that without understanding *sola scriptura*, Martin Luther would have lacked the nerve to levy his protests against the Roman Catholic Church. At that point in time, Rome held everyone captive by fear—fear that they had not done enough for the Church and for God to warrant salvation. The Roman Catholic Church and the Pope were impenetrable forces—or at least they thought they were. Rome declared that the traditions of the Church had the same authority as the text of Scripture. Therefore, if you didn't bow the knee to the papacy and obey their laws along with God's Law, you were taking your eternal life into your own hands.

Can you imagine the fear Luther felt when he posted those now famous 95 theses in Wittenberg? If he were wrong he would be damned to Hell. (Side note, that's exactly what happened to Luther. According to the Catholic Church, Luther is in Hell for rejecting the Pope's authority.) As frightful as posting that note must have been, Luther had confidence he was right. It was clear that Rome had confused grace with works. In Rome's understanding, the sinner needed the Church. This need went far beyond the unity, support, and exhortation that is described in Scripture as the purpose for the Church. Rather, Rome declared that without it you could not be reconciled to God. The Church thought it held the keys to eternal life. Luther discovered this was clearly against the teaching of Scripture. The Gospel is "by grace through faith." The cooperation that Rome required, along with grace, was simply anti-gospel.

When we say *sola scriptura* today, it is most often used to mean inerrancy, the doctrine which declares the Bible to be without error in all its teaching. Or specifically that "Scripture in the original manuscripts does not affirm anything that is contrary to fact." This of course is true: the Bible is inerrant. But inerrancy wasn't the struggle Luther had with the Church, because both he and the Church agreed on that reality. Both understood the Bible to be God's words. The real struggle Luther faced concerned how to deal with the additional sources of truth. What happens when these extra-biblical sources contradict each other? Who gets the final say? In Luther's time the Church, traditions, and the Pope received that final vote. The Pope could clearly contradict Scripture—and it was OK. Luther called these actions on the carpet. It was clear to him that Scripture alone held the final authority. If someone, or something, contradicted the clear teaching of Scripture, they would be wrong, and Scripture would be right. In its simplest form, *sola scriptura* is the declaration that the Church can err. Luther's message was clear—just because you call yourself the Church doesn't mean you can oppose the clear teaching of Scripture.

With this understanding, Luther had the guts to question

the frightening spiritual machine the Church had become. Theologian Kevin Vanhoozer describes this moment:

> *The legitimacy of the Reformation stands or falls*
> *on Luther's judgment that Scripture alone contains*
> *all things necessary for salvation, communicates*
> *them effectively, compels one's conscience, determines*
> *doctrinal truth, and commands the church's allegiance*
> *above all other earthly powers and authorities,*
> *including councils and popes.*

The greatest threat to the Roman Catholic Church was the Bible! Luther, from the platform of "Scripture alone" was able to take on this historic system—and win. For centuries the Medieval Church had a lock on the souls of men. Luther broke that lock and released the common man from the bonds of the Catholic Church. Luther rediscovered that man didn't *need* Rome or the Pope to be saved. He saw the clear teaching of the Bible—salvation is through faith. In short, Luther realized that the overarching point of Scripture is to declare how sinful individuals can be reconciled to a holy God. At one point, Luther approached the Bible to learn "what" to do, but this proved to be a weapon of despair in his life. In the end, Luther came to see Scripture as a book declaring what God did to redeem mankind from the bondage of sin. It was a message of grace.

We owe a lot to Luther for this recovered understanding of Scripture. But one of the biggest ironies of the Reformation is that what gave Luther the confidence to question the Church has now been identified as the "sin of the Reformation." Vanhoozer states further, "[*Sola scriptura*] is the doctrine that opened up what we have described as the Pandora's box of Protestantism, namely, the unchecked subjectivism that follows from the assumptions that the text of Scripture makes sense separate from the Church that gives it sense." Before the Reformation, Rome controlled the meaning of Scripture and traditions, and there was no place for contradictory biblical views. But when Luther declared "Scripture alone" as the final authority, it opened up the possibility for any person to sit alone with a Bible and determine what it means—a possibility that has changed the face of the Church. The *one face* of the Catholic Church has now been exchanged for the *many faces* of Protestant denominations.

We live in this confusion. Consider the local churches in your area. Every Sunday pastors present the same passages of Scripture to their congregations, often with conflicting meanings. For many congregations there is no unifying purpose and point of the Bible holding it all together. Though the majority of these churches hold to Luther's declaration of *sola scriptura* as a central tenet of their faith, they make a common mistake. Instead of viewing the Bible as the *final authority*, they see Scripture as the *only authority*. Or to say it another way, the declaration of *sola scriptura* (Scripture alone) is understood to mean *solo scriptura* (Scripture only). It's assumed that the *only* resource a believer needs is a specific text of Scripture. With just that, an individual is able to interpret and determine the meaning and application for each particular passage they read. Those who hold to this position are called *Biblicists*. "If the Bible says it, I believe it." As one author states, "Biblicists see theology as essentially an individual project whereby the reader exegetes a handful of passages and then makes theological conclusions." As long as a Bible verse can be interpreted to agree with your position, you're good to go. The Bible is then turned into a giant "proof text", split up into "nuggets of truth" and thrown about with no clear structure. This again is why the redemptive-historical view of Scripture is so important. It protects us from wandering off into heresy. The Bible is a tool that needs to be handled appropriately. If you don't know where the "on" switch is, the Bible will return, once again, into an overwhelming weapon of despair.

It's Sad How Common This Is

Let me illustrate this despair I keep referencing. Think about the majority of evangelical sermons. The message regularly preached is: "God wants you to change your actions" and "Stop sinning and glorify God." The Church's major campaign has become improving the believer's actions and habits through the direction of God's Word. The biblical characters are the primary moral examples, pastors are the master drill sergeants, and the congregants are their cadets in training. "Worship like David," " believe with the same intensity as Abraham," and "love like Jesus," has become the weekly mantra. There is a call to action every time the Bible is opened. *Do this. Don't do that.* The "lists" offered are torture devices for sinners and pride-builders for the self-righteous and self-made. Evangelicalism, and specifically pietism, are systems based on measuring up. For some the Christian life is about becoming *better.* The aim is to increase your morality, with the Bible being a book of laws where every ethic is laid out as our judge. Under this system the expectation for the Christian is to progressively fulfill God's commands. With God's word being the standard, the Christian must go from a five to a seven on the scale of morality.

Ever wonder why your pastor always sounds disgusted? It could be because you're not measuring up. You're not moving up the scale fast enough. This type of preacher has been described by R. Scott Clark as a "legal preacher."

> *A legal preacher is a preacher who majors in the law to the neglect of the gospel. In practice, he preaches nothing but law. He thinks that mentioning Jesus periodically or even regularly means that he's not a legal preacher... He turns every passage into a law, because he doesn't know any other way to read the Scripture and he doesn't know any other way to preach. He preaches the law and he doesn't even know he's doing it, even when, in his mind, he's preaching the gospel. When he finds a bit of good news in his passage, he doesn't end with that because he doesn't*

want his people to get the idea that there are no obligations to the Christian life.

I also believe there is such a thing as a "legal reader." Are you never satisfied with your Christian "walk?" Are you always trying to attain the standard that the Bible puts forward as the markers you have to achieve? Have you found that no matter how much you read, meditate, memorize, or recite, you just can't keep the standard? If so, you're probably a "legal reader." Don't worry, you got here honestly. Pietism indoctrinates followers into a merit-based system of approval with the Bible being the chief judge. It's no wonder so many people find the Bible to be the most tiresome part of the Christian life.

Maybe I just described your relationship with the Bible. If so, allow me to refocus your attention back to the amazing storyline of the Bible.

The Story

A fact hiding in the wide-open is that the Bible is first a story. Stories are at the heart of what it means to be human. And there are few mediums more captivating than a well-told story. No one ever complains about being swept up and mentally transported away by the stories of another. The same excitement of hearing a Berenstain Bears story as a child is still there when someone starts recounting a personal event around the campfire later in life. Young or old, stories entice us all. It's in our nature to lean forward and listen intently.

Growing up, I hated reading. It's a common thread with many boys. The last thing I wanted was to sit inside with my nose in a book. But then at twelve, I received a series called *The Home Ranch*. It was a story about a young boy in the West who went to work on a ranch. And, as all good stories go, he became the hero and saved the day. It was a long series, or at least it looked long to my twelve-year-old self. But I devoured each book, reading a hundred pages a day. I'd get caught up in the story and not want to put it down. And when it was over, I read each book again. The more I read, the better I understood the storyline. And the better I understood the storyline, the more I read. I was compelled to read because I was attracted by the story. At that point in my life I wanted to be that kid in the West. I wanted his story to be my story. That connection drew me back to read the whole series several times.

For a believer, the Bible is a compelling story because we're included in the story. Scripture is the story of how sinners can be offered hope. In the midst of our unworthiness, it answers the question "How can we become good with God." It explains not only what God requires, but also how He fulfilled the requirements. This might be a completely new reality to you. This story may have been so convoluted over the years that you can't even imagine a story that offers hope, and not more work.

The story of the Bible sounds the same to us as it did to every individual found in Scripture; an announcement that there is good news. It's the story about how God, before the foundation of the world determined to save the world. It's the story of our reconciliation.

The Main Characters

To truly understand any story you have to understand the main characters. The Bible is a tale of two Adams. It's paramount to understand how these two Adams fit into the flow. Their actions affect us all. What happens to them happens to us. Theologically speaking, this is called federal headship. Federal headship has to do with representation, where one person acts on behalf of another. These two "Adams" are our representatives before God.

The first Adam is the man we meet in the garden. Adam was offered the promise of eternal life through obeying God's Law. The standard was perfection. Any deviation from God's holy Law was not acceptable. While this standard is impossible for us today, Adam, being created morally upright, had every ability to complete this command and obtain the promise. This standard was important for several reasons. First, the creature has the obligation to obey the Creator. But secondly, being our federal representative for all of man, it was all riding on him. Adam was the legal representative of all his posterity. As the *London Baptist Confession* describes:

> *God gave to Adam a law of universal obedience*
> *written in his heart, and a particular precept of not*
> *eating the fruit of the tree of knowledge of good and*
> *evil; by which he bound him and all his posterity*

to personal, entire, exact, and perpetual obedience;
promised life upon the fulfilling, and threatened
death upon the breach of it, and endued him with
power and ability to keep it.

Unfortunately, Adam did not fulfill what was required. He broke the law. He sinned. Thus incurring guilt and condemnation for him and for all his descendants. Sin and death are now the inherited and imputed attributes upon every descendant of Adam. In addition to sin and death, Adam lost access to God. Prior to sin, Adam communed with God. He had access to his Creator because nothing stood in the way. Now, with the presence of sin and guilt, man cannot freely access our Creator. As Ephesians 2:12 declares:

Remember that you were at that time separated from
Christ, alienated from the commonwealth of Israel
and strangers to the covenants of promise, having no
hope and without God in the world.

The presence of God now brings fear and dread. We no longer run toward our God, rather we run from him in fear (Exodus 20:18-20). Adam left mankind in a desperate state. The guilt of his sin infected us all, and there is no way we can undo the sin and fulfill what is required.

This is where the second Adam enters the story. The second Adam was uniquely qualified. He was truly human, being born of a woman. Therefore He had the ability to fulfill what the first Adam could not. But He was also truly God, so He did not inherit Adam's guilt. There was now a second Adam on earth, a man who had the ability to fulfill God's law and earn what was lost by the first Adam. This man had the ability to finally offer hope.

I'm sure you know the end of the story. This second Adam, the man we know as Christ, did just that. He came and lived a perfect life. He kept the whole Law—every part, with no exceptions. As Hebrews 3:15 states, "he fulfilled all righteousness." In Romans 5, Paul describes these two Adams and their actions: "For as by a man came death, by a man has come also the resurrection of the dead. For as in Adam all die, so also in Christ shall all be made alive."

Behind the tale of two Adams is the doctrine of imputation. Taken directly from Latin, imputation is an accounting term meaning, "to apply to one's account." This doctrine cannot go unnoticed in Scripture. It's first seen with Adam in the garden, it continues with the sacrificial lamb at Passover, and finally concludes with Christ. Our standing before God has always been based upon the consequences of another. Just as Adam's guilt was imputed to us, so too, Christ's righteousness can be imputed to us "by grace through faith." But imputation also goes the other direction. In addition to Christ's righteousness being imputed to us, our unrighteousness was imputed to him on the Cross. Christ's death paid the penalty for our sins. God's wrath against our guilt and condemnation was satisfied in Christ on the Cross.

Christ accomplished everything necessary for us to be reconciled to a holy God. Second Corinthians 5:21 declares: "For our sake he made him to be sin who knew no sin, so that in him we might become the righteousness of God." If you miss these two Adams, you're going to miss the central focus of this story. These two men give us the framework for the story of redemption. They tell us what we need to know about the Gospel. Focusing on them keeps the central story of redemption clear. If you boil everything down in the Bible, these two Adams are the bones underneath it all.

Where We Go Wrong

As we've said, the story of redemption can be a challenge to keep in focus. The Bible contains a vast amount of narrative and history, which is essential for the progression of the story. But narrative, and especially history, isn't always flashy. It can be hard for people to be compelled simply by dialogue. For many, the common Bible-reading strategy follows three simple steps: Read. Observe. Apply. Every time they sit down with Scripture, they read the passage, observe what it has to say, and apply the details to their life. There are some parts of Scripture where this plan is hard to execute, and these become the most ignored parts of Scripture. In order to use the three-step method in the narratives of the Bible, the story of redemption is diminished and the characters God used to push the storyline along are promoted. These characters have usurped their intended role. The story of two Adams has been transformed into a story emphasizing the supporting characters.

The deviation away from the story of redemption is commonly caused by unnecessarily moralizing the lives and actions of these biblical characters. The assumption is often, "if they're in the Bible, they can do no wrong." Or, "if God used them, we should follow in their footsteps." We regularly point to every one of God's servants and say, "Try to be like them." We go so far as to say that our daughters need to be women like Esther. This is wrong! Go read her story and consider how she got her title as queen. It wasn't a Miss America pageant she was in. I would be heartbroken to find my girls following in her footsteps. We see redemption not through her "godly" actions, but through her weakness. God used a woman known for her "dancing" to push the story of redemption along. When we spend so much time determining how all the stories apply directly to us, we miss Christ entirely.

This focus minimizes the beauty of Scripture. I get it, it's difficult for finite minds to grasp how God can shape and expand a singular story over hundreds of generations. But that's just what God did. Changing the focus and purpose of these stories is nothing new. It's exactly what liberal critics from the eighteenth and nineteenth centuries did. By questioning and later denying the divine authorship of Scripture, they stripped the Bible of all objective authority. For them, the Bible was simply a group of stories telling about the history of ancient Israel. By removing the overarching continuity between the stories, critics sought to disprove that God actually had a plan for Scripture. Once the overarching story and continuity was gone, they easily eliminated all authority that the Bible inherently has.

I hope by now you see the importance of the redemptive-historical view. Understanding this theme can be the needed guideline that keeps us from tipping off into heresy. When reading the Bible, don't forget about the continuity in the story. Your mind will be blown away by the detail and descriptions God gave us throughout Scripture. God told the story of the Bible in a specific way for a specific reason. We might not always understand it at first glance, but God had a divine plan when he rolled out the story of redemption. As Graeme Goldsworthy wisely states,

> *Who of us does not find at least some parts of the Bible difficult to understand? It is easy to ignore the problems by keeping to the well-worn paths of familiar passages. But when we begin to take seriously the fact that the whole Bible is the Word of God, we find ourselves on a collision path with difficulties. It is at this point that we need biblical theology [redemptive-historical view] to show us how to read and understand the Bible.*

The Bible is truly a story fashioned by God, written with the hands of forty men, spanning thousands of years, in three different languages, to explain one simple point: We can be saved!

The Story Unpacked

Allow me to illustrate the redemptive-historical view in action. Have you ever considered the purpose of the Exodus? Why did God allow His people to go into Egypt, fall into captivity, be saved by ten plagues, freed, trapped at the shores of the Red Sea, wander the wilderness for forty years, and then finally make it to the Jordan River? Why put Israel through all that heartache? This is God we're talking about. He could have miraculously teleported everyone anywhere He wanted. He could have kept them out of Egypt in the first place. There must have been an easier way.

It's a valid question. Many have attempted to supply a sufficient answer. These answers range from it being God's first attempt to create His kingdom on earth, to God's judgment of sin; and some even go so far to say that the Exodus experience is an example believers need to follow to properly live as children of God in a sinful world. But the only way to see the real purpose of the Exodus is to look forward to the events in the New Testament. By placing the events of the Old Testament in light of the reality of the New Testament, you can accurately understand what's going during this forty-year period.

The Exodus was given so we can better understand what happened to us in Christ. You see, God uses pictures, analogies, types, and shadows in the Old Testament so we can better understand what's going on in the New Testament. We were given the *shadows* so we could better recognize the *Substance* when He arrived. This is what we mean when we talk about continuity in Scripture. The writer of Hebrews is referring to this continuity when he declared:

> *Long ago, at many times and in many ways, God spoke to our fathers by the prophets, but in these last days he has spoken to us by his Son, whom he appointed the heir of all things, through whom also he created the world.* (Hebrews 1:1-2)

The *shadows* in the Old Testament give greater clarity of the realities in the New Testament. With the story of redemption fulfilled in Christ, we can look back and learn from these events in a different way. We now see that the Exodus was more than God physically saving and giving His people the Promised Land. It's an analogy of what God does with every person reconciled to God.

Consider where the Exodus story begins. Israel was stuck in captivity. Its people were held in a state of complete bondage. But God stepped in and graciously freed them for no other reason than the fact that He had determined to save His chosen people. Now consider this in Ephesians:,

> *You were dead in the trespasses and sins ... But God, being rich in mercy, because of the great love with which he loved us, even when we were dead in our trespasses, made us alive together with Christ—by grace you have been saved.* (Ephesians 2:1,4-5)

Our deliverance from our bondage of sin shares the same reason as Israel's deliverance from the bondage of Egypt—grace.

But the analogy continues. By crossing the Red Sea they entered into the *already not yet* reality of the wilderness experience. They were no longer in the bondage of slavery, but had yet to arrive in the Promised Land. The children of Israel struggled to rest in their freedom. They were free but didn't feel free. We follow the very same path. We are saved by "the washing of regeneration" and "become heirs according to the hope of eternal life" (Titus 3:5-7). But like Abraham, we are still waiting for the Promised Land (Hebrews 11:9-10). We still feel like we are in bondage to sin even though we are free.

This is just one piece of clarity that is found in the Old Testament. The list can go on and on: the pillar of cloud and fire, the elements of the tabernacle, the sacrifices, the promises of God—they all point to Christ. They all give greater clarity to the redemptive storyline. This is what excited and spurred on the apostles and disciples in the early Church. Stephen's sermon in Acts 7 serves as a great example of the redemptive-historical view promoted in Scripture. As the Church grew and the message of the Gospel spread, the religious leaders questioned how Christ could be the promised Messiah. Stephen's response was plain and simple. He systematically walked through the Old Testament, starting with Abraham and ending with the prophets, and showed how they all pointed to Christ. The biblical characters understood *they* were not the point of the Bible, but rather it was about the coming Messiah. The characters of the Old Testament had one purpose: to point toward Christ.

Before we move on, one quick note about this sermon from Stephen. Consider how this encounter ended. Luke tells us when Stephen was done, "They were enraged, and they ground their teeth at him.... Then they cast him out of the city and stoned him." Don't let this detail pass by unnoticed. When the religious people heard that Christ is the point of the Old Testament and all the faithful characters were there to point to someone greater, this brought them to a rage. The religious leaders had been trying to live up to the life of David, Moses, Abraham. Their standing in religious society, not to mention their standing before God, was tied to how well they could impersonate the great biblical characters of old. They undoubtedly and painstakingly arranged their lives to mimic the principles they saw in the men who went before them. Now they were hearing those principles and platitudes did not matter before God. Even if you did a perfect impression of Moses, it was not enough to merit salvation. This is deflating. This is depressing. No! This is infuriating! If they believed Stephen, their entire life's work and religious pursuit would be for naught. They could not allow that to be true and so their response was to kill the messenger and hope that the reality of the message would die with him.

What stands out most in Stephen's story is that the first time a person promoted the redemptive-historical view in a religious culture, he was quickly put to death. While obviously I have not died for promoting this view, but I have experienced the anger it can cause. At this point in history many have slipped back into pointing people toward the faithfulness of the secondary biblical characters and not the faithfulness of Christ. Many have spent their life trying to be a man like David, a leader like Nehemiah, a faithful women like Esther, and pray like Jabez. It is an offensive reality to tell someone his or her life's spiritual work is worthless for salvation. If you follow Stephen's teaching, be prepared to dodge a few stones now and again.

Conclusion

The fact is, God used forty men, over thousands of years, in three different languages to explain one simple truth—humans can be reconciled to a holy God. It is the only truth broad enough to include everything, yet specific enough to define it. The Bible is the unabridged message of God's relentless grace toward unworthy sinners. Don't lose sight of this reality. Don't forget to use the "on" switch when you pick up this tool. I pray every time you approach the Bible, your faith is strengthened through a better understanding of this amazing story. Still don't believe me? Go read it for yourself.

CHAPTER FIVE

Why the Struggle?

What is your prayer life like? When is the last time you prayed? How often are you praying? How long are you praying? Now, what emotion are you feeling at the moment? Do you feel guilty? If you are like me, your lack of consistency leads you to guilt. Guilt was that constant shadow that trailed my prayer life. Guilt is what motivated me to try harder. Prayer felt like an endless cycle: *guilt, try harder, guilt, try harder.* And when I still saw no answers to my prayer requests, the guilt piled up even more. I assumed no answer meant I didn't have enough faith.

Let me ask you another question: Why do you think most Christians struggle to pray? I recently posted this question on a Twitter survey. Almost one hundred and fifty people responded to four options. The results were interesting:

50% No Discipline

9% Unanswered Prayer

24% Doesn't Feel Natural

17% Not Clear on the Purpose

Which would you choose? What is the root cause of your struggle with prayer? For most of my life, I would have picked "no discipline." But once I started to look at the Christian life from a reformed, non-pietistic perspective, I learned the actual reason I struggled. A.W. Pink wrote,:"[In our prayers,] the human elements fill the scene almost entirely: it is the conditions which we must meet, the promises we must claim, the things we must do to get our requests granted." Do you see the operative focus in Pink's point? "Us." To guarantee an answer to our prayers, we must continuously be examining our dedication, excitement, attrition, repentance, or longevity. We seek after instructions and inspiration to help us stay focused and progress in our pursuit of a successful prayer life. We read biographies of victorious prayer warriors, attend prayer conferences, listen to podcasts, read books, blogs, etc. Prayer plans that promise success seems to come in all shapes and sizes, and yet most of them focus on what we are to do.

What are we seeking in this pursuit? We are trying to find relief from guilt. We hate questions related to our prayer life. We read Paul's instructions to us that we should "pray without ceasing," and the only part of us that doesn't seem to "cease" is our guilt. You are most likely feeling it in this chapter. You're probably thinking, "*The solution to my lifelong struggle with prayer is only a few paragraphs away. There is a flicker of hope just around the corner, just one more page away.*" Spoiler alert! You will not find it in this chapter, or any book that's ever been written. I offer no key to a successful prayer life. What I can offer is an explanation of how we came to hold this introspective view and why it's contrary to the message of the Gospel and why prayer leads us to guilt instead of delight. Here are three examples of ways we approach God in prayer that only lead to despair instead of hope:

Appeasement

A familiar refrain we hear thrown around is that God disciplines those He loves. And while the phrase might be biblical, it's often incorrectly taken to mean that the loss of a job, a car accident, and busted pipes are all possible examples of God trying to get our attention. What is the solution that is offered? "Pray forty-five minutes a day and God will remove these circumstances from your life." OK, it doesn't sound exactly like that—but it's underneath. When something goes wrong, we blame it on our lack of prayer that day, week, month. If we had kept God happy with our devotion to Him, He would have prevented these problems. Keep Him happy, and you will have fewer problems.

In the Ancient Near East, pagan worshipers would present

sacrifices to appease their gods. No rain? They believed that the gods required sacrifices to calm their anger and release the rain. Still no answer? The gods must desire a costlier sacrifice. How does this translate? If you equate time spent in prayer to God's protection, you are approaching God in the same fashion as the pagans do their gods.

I have personally seen this approach to prayer confuse and discourage many believers. They felt that their current situation was the result of letting their payments lapse in "God's protection plan." When I receive these emails, my response is always the same! Cancer, car accidents, loss of a job, debt, depression, etc., are not the result of an angry God expressing His disapproval of your lack of dedication.

Favor

Favor is similar to appeasement, except that you are servicing God's demands to receive a blessing rather than to prevent calamity. Success in raising your kids, your job, relationships, and so on, is directly tied to how much time you have spent in prayer. God's blessings flow down to those who are faithful. You could almost say God pays most attention to those who pay most attention to Him. The famous Bible verse from James is flippantly taken out of context and used in this line of thinking, "you have not because you ask not." The way it's used can almost sound like, "Convince God you really want it, He will eventually see it your way."

Something is intriguing about the concept of finding the faucet to the storehouses of God. Who wouldn't want to learn how to turn on the streams of blessings? We as Christians have been convinced that we must pray in certain positions, locations, lengths, without food, walking, lying down, early, late, quiet, loud, laughing, and crying. The promised result? That with the right method, God would open His ear to your request, and you would receive blessings unmeasurable. These prayer techniques sound like sales pitches on *Shark Tank*. You merely need to convince God that you have a good system and He needs to partner with you. If He does, you will make His brand more appealing to those who lack faith. When none of these methods seem to work, you are told that you didn't try it long enough, you didn't have enough faith, and you even might have unconfessed sin. In other words, like appeasement, it depends on you.

Filling Station

This last approach is similar to the previous two but camouflaged in a more traditional and biblical format. The amount of time we spend in prayer fills us with spiritual fuel preparing us for the trials and temptations we face each day. Did you snap at the kids? Were you short with your spouse or co-worker? Did you cuss at a bad driver in front of you? Did you fall back into anxiety, doubt, or depression? Did lust win again today? You must have left that day with an empty tank. Prayer is just an energy drink to give you the spiritual boost you need to fight sin and temptation. Without prayer, our hearts and minds don't have the energy to resist the seductions of Satan. Beginning each day in prayer calibrates us so that we are spiritually prepared to face the trials of the day. If we skip a day, guilt begins to cloud our mind. Any sin or struggle we fall into is quickly seen as our lack of commitment to prayer that morning. Prayer is how we put on our daily armor. It is how we spiritually fill ourselves and grow.

What could be wrong with this? I'm not too sure I agree with you. The first two may have seemed ridiculous, but now it sounds as if you are disagreeing with the Bible. This is why I said it is camouflaged. It appears biblical, but underneath it is pure pietism. Prayer is reduced down to a transaction. We provide God the required actions, He gives blessings and protection. The moment you put faith in your performance, even if it is prayer, you are living by faithfulness and not faith. You are approaching prayer like a lucky rabbit's foot or spiritual airborne. This is not to say that there are not benefits of spending time daily in prayer, but to equate your success or failures with this time spent is actually opposed to the Gospel.

Where Did We Go Wrong?

Over the last four hundred years, Christianity has slowly slipped away from a reformed understanding of *sola fide*, or a life lived by faith alone in Christ, and has embraced a hybrid of Roman Catholic mysticism and evangelicalism. We commonly confess that we are saved by grace through faith alone, but we betray this reality when we place the responsibility of sanctification back on the faithfulness of the believer. We are told that sanctification is achieved through what is called "spiritual disciplines." Don Whitney, who has written extensively on this subject, describes them as "practices found in Scripture that promote spiritual growth among believers in the gospel of Jesus Christ. They are habits of devotion, habits of experiential Christianity."

This brings up an important question: What is the most essential spiritual discipline for the Christian life? Prayer? Devotions? Meditation? I've asked this question to a number of Christians, and while everyone's lists are different, there is one glaring similarity: No one ever says, "faith!" I think there is a good explanation as to why. Until the 1970s, it was difficult to find any popular materials or teachers endorsing the subject of spiritual disciplines. Beginning in the early '70s and '80s men such as Richard Foster and Dallas Willard gave this movement sustained credibility. More recently, Donald Whitney in his book, *Spiritual Disciplines for the Christian Life*, has caused even greater confusion by tying his method to reformed theology. This is the very medieval spirituality that the reformers opposed. It has been introduced back into Christianity and infiltrated the majority of books written on prayer. Richard Foster, who is considered to be the father of the modern spiritual disciplines movement wrote:

> *When I first began writing in the field in the late 70s and early 80s the term 'Spiritual Formation' was*

hardly known, except for highly specialized references in relation to the Catholic orders. (Spiritual Formation: A Pastoral Letter, Richard Foster)

The influence of men like Foster, Willard, and Whitney has changed the way we understand the purpose and practice of spiritual disciplines. Ask any Christian if they have heard of the concept of spiritual disciplines and most likely they will give you a short list of required actions which lead to spiritual growth and protection.

So, there you have it. When did this introspective view of prayer in modern Christianity get its wings? It happened the moment the focus shifted from what God has done for us, to what we should be doing for God.

What Is the Purpose of Prayer?

Have you ever thought about what is actually happening when you pray? What you're admitting at that very moment? You're acknowledging your need of something outside of yourself. You recognize your need for something you cannot provide. Likewise, you are accepting the sufficiency of God to supply the very need you are requesting. The very nature of prayer is dependence. When we reach the end of our rope, when the last thread of hope is gone, where do we turn? Prayer! *If there is a God, I need your help now!* We are depending on His power because we are powerless at the moment. But, we are always powerless. We are always in need. It is only in these moments of despair, we finally recognize our creatureliness.

So, what is the purpose of prayer? Dependence. Prayer is transferring our dependency into the loving hands of the Father. Martin Luther saw prayer to be "*the conversation of the dependent and trusting child, who is eager to voice both thanks and requests with the loving Father, who in turn is eager to hear from His children.*" Luther doesn't see God as one to be appeased, but trusted. God's favor is not earned, but inherited as children. This dependence frees us to cry out to Him when we are in pain, shout for joy when we receive His blessings, openly repent and find endless forgiveness when sin deceives us yet again, boldly seek wisdom when confused, and find rest when we are weary.

This change in perspective has transformed the way I approach prayer. Before, prayer was always a chore because all I could ever see was God holding back His protection and blessings unless I, in a sense, played the game. Prayer felt more like a *duty* than a *privilege. I must pray*, instead of, *I get to pray*. If you are always attempting to appease Him, fill up your protection bank, or earn His favor, it will be almost impossible to visualize prayer as a privilege. This is where the Law and Gospel have been confused. Prayer has been transferred over to the Law category. Prayer is required if we are to be accepted as righteous before God, or gain His favor. The longer and more intensely you pray, the more God will be pleased with you. We have moved a gift that flows from the Gospel into a Law. This gift is a way to express our pain and joy. It isn't a ladder to work our way into His favor, but an armchair to lean into His presence. He says, *Come, and express your deepest pains and desires to me.* Hebrews 4:15 reads, "For we do not have a high priest who is unable to sympathize with our weaknesses, but one who in every respect has been tempted as we are, yet without sin." We have no reason to fear God turning His ear away from our cries of pain and frustration. He never told us, "I'll love you if you do better." His unconditional love draws us near, and He patiently listens to our struggles, our rejoicing, our crying, and our repentance. The purpose of prayer is to spend time with God, to whom we look to for everything in this life. We are the ones who benefit from this gift. We are the ones who receive the joy of refreshing our souls in the glory of our redemption. Prayer is not what we can do for God. Prayer is reminding ourselves that He is what we need.

Recalibrating Prayer

Once you dip your toe into the waters of reformed theology, your entire world begins to recalibrate. What was once a requirement is now an invitation to experience God's love in full color. What used to be a burden is now a weightless experience. Prayer fits into this category of *delight* instead of *dread.* The gospel removes the confusion and clarifies the glorious experience of prayer. Prayer changes from being a requirement for God's grace, to granting unlimited access to God's grace— from complicated and confusing, to simple and refreshing. The moment you realize that the effectiveness of prayer is never the result of personal performance, it sounds almost too good to be true. Before this can happen, we must recalibrate your thinking as it relates to the Gospel and prayer.

The Gospel and Prayer

As stated earlier, the doctrine of *sola fide* that was regained in the Reformation five hundred years ago, is once again slowly slipping away. The doctrine is at the core of the Gospel—God declares sinners righteous by grace alone through faith alone. The perfect life Jesus lived, His righteousness, and His status, are now our life, our righteousness, our status in the eyes of God (Romans 3:21-22; 1 Corinthians 1:30). He calls us "child." We call Him "Daddy" ("*Abba! Father!*" Romans 8:15). He is well pleased with us. Nothing we do can separate us from our adoption, His grace, or His love. The love the Father has for His children is special and unique. He has expressed the same love for us as His children as He does Jesus, His only Son (John 17:20-24). That means all children at all times are equally receiving the affections of the Father as Christ receives them. This is done because God has willed it to be, not because we have earned it (John 1:12-13).

God has made right all that we have corrupted and rebelled against. This includes our prayers. If you are declared justified by the Father, your prayers are included. Your prayers are accepted on the merits of Jesus' righteousness. The Father listens to every word you say—all of them! They don't reach His throne room in the voice of Charlie Brown's parents because we failed to meet the right requirements. The requirements already have been achieved by Christ, and we are called to come boldly into His presence and talk to Him as Father (Hebrews 4:16).

The Gospel brings the purpose of prayer back into focus for us. As one popular author wrote, "Prayer is not trying to persuade God to do something He otherwise would not do. It is our being caught up in the purposes of God and expression of this privilege as His dear children who know Him as Father." The Father knows what we need, and willingly wants to give it to us. Often, we assume that our prayer life suffers due to the lack of our intensity. This is a focus on us and not on Christ. All too often believers struggle with their assurance because they don't see a strong desire or practice of prayer. The author continues, "The genuineness of faith is always defined by its object, not its intensity." We always will be accepted by the Father on faith alone. The Gospel always should be what fuels our desire for prayer.

The Single Greatest Enemy to Prayer?

Have you ever thought, *Why does God not answer me?* Ask five Christians this question and you will get seven different answers. Biblicism (which is the tendency to appeal to individual verses or a collection of uniform verses, ignoring the greater context) reigns supreme when it comes to how God answers prayer. The go-to American answer sounds something like: "You have not because you ask not." Another popular example would be: "Whatever you ask in my name, believe, and it will be yours." Probably my favorite misunderstood passage is when Jesus gives an illustration right after teaching His disciples about prayer. Jesus tells a story about a man who had guests staying with him late at night but had no food to provide for them. In the middle of the night, the host runs to his neighbor's house to ask for food for his guests. At the end of the story, Jesus said, "Because of his persistence ... he will give him whatever he needs." (Luke 11:8) If you ignore the surrounding context of this verse (which is Biblicism), one can only conclude that God will not answer your prayer unless: 1) You remember to ask; 2) You ask with enough faith; and 3) You ask a lot.

It is hard to argue with these verses when they appear to be so clear and straightforward. Pietistic teaching has become embedded in the roots of our thinking concerning prayer. We hear stories of people who have seen incredible answers to prayer because they "asked a lot." The stories seem genuine. How can you argue with results? So we ask God for hundreds of requests to only see one answered and conclude, *we did something right, how do we repeat it?* Doesn't that seem odd? Does anyone else struggle with how the Bible promises to answer all of our requests, yet we only see one in a hundred? The promise from Jesus in Mark 11:24 is that if we ask for anything—with faith—He will give it to us. Did we only have enough faith to see one in a hundred prayers answered? Is the problem really not enough faith?

We assume we are reading a passage at face value, allowing the text to speak for itself, when in reality we are placing our own pietistic grid over it. What seems plain and simple only appears this way because of how we have been taught for our entire lives. My brain just doesn't work that way. If something seems out of place, I want to know why. I've tried every modern method of prayer in my lifetime. Each system sounds biblical and uses a lot of Bible verses, but in the end...every prayer is not being answered as promised by Jesus.

Is it just me? I've been in ministry long enough to know "unanswered prayers" are more common than answered prayers. I would say the most significant reason most Christians struggle with prayer is that they don't really see any legitimate answers to their requests. It's understandable. Would you drive every day to the bank to withdraw cash if you knew there was no money in the bank? Of course not. What if I told you there was an endless supply of money and you can take what you need for the day. You would make that ten-minute drive without thinking twice. In other words, prayer seems like the empty bank account. You have made the drive, but walk away empty-handed too many times. Maybe it's time we attempt to clear our minds of the systems that have failed us in the past and see what it is that God has given us in this gift called prayer.

How Should We Pray?

It all comes down to willpower! Did your stomach turn just a little when you read that statement? It's a true statement, just not in the way you think. The *Westminster Shorter Catechism* states:

"What is prayer? A. Prayer is an offering up of our desires unto God, for things agreeable to His will, in the name of Christ, with confession of our sins, and thankful acknowledgment of His mercies." God's will is unstoppable. Isaiah 46:10 reads: "Declaring the end from the beginning and from ancient times things not yet done, saying, 'My counsel shall stand, and I will accomplish all my purpose." And Proverbs 19:21: "Many are the plans in the mind of a man, but it is the purpose of the LORD that will stand." If God will not bend His desires to the desires of humans, it would seem logical that there would be millions of unanswered prayers. By in large, the desires of humanity contradict God's desires. Do humans hit the prayer lottery once in a while and ask for something that aligns with God's plan of redemption? It would appear so because we hear and read numerous stories of God answering people's prayers. The church in Acts prayed for Peter's release from prison. Moses petitioned God to spare His wrath against the children of Israel. The Prophet Elijah's prayer brought a dead boy back to life. Why is this not the norm? Why do some experience answers to prayer and others do not? Is it truly just a matter of spiritual luck?

Thankfully, Christ did not leave us in the dark. He gave us a clear view into the storehouses of heaven through a simple little lesson given to His disciples. Jesus' prayer habits the disciples observed were very different than what they had experienced in their lifetime. So much so, that they asked Jesus to teach them. What was it that Jesus had to teach them? How hard is it to stop and have a simple conversation with God? Were they that ignorant of who God was and His abilities? We should not underestimate these fishermen: they were well-taught Jews who knew the Torah. What did they lack in their understanding of prayer that they wanted to be taught? Access. The illustrative, unabated life. They witnessed a Son talk to His Father—an act entirely foreign in their religious experience. Jesus didn't tell them what they needed to say as if their problem was their format. He forever altered their relationship with God in prayer. They had a new level of access to the Father never before seen. Jesus opens a whole new world with one little phrase: "Our Father." No one in the history of the world ever claimed such a personal title concerning God. D.A. Carson wrote: "The fatherhood of God is not a central theme in the Old Testament. Where "father" does occur with respect to God, it is commonly by way of analogy, not direct address (Deuteronomy 32:6; Psalms 103:13; Isaiah 63:16; Malachi 2:10)." It is easy to see how this would blow a circuit in the mind of a well-trained Jew. The Torah never encourages the Israelites to claim such intimacy with God. Carson continues, "There is no evidence of anyone before Jesus using this term to address God... This opening designation establishes the kind of God to whom prayer is offered... That He is "our Father" establishes the relationship that exists between Jesus' disciples and God."

Not only did they have access to God in ways they had never seen before, but they were also approaching Him as a son.

They were being granted the same access as THE Son of God. Jesus had just introduced something completely foreign to their religious context. He assumed a close relational proximity to God, and upon that relationship, made what would appear to be familial requests. What they heard Jesus teaching them was their right to claim sonship to God. This would have felt dangerous and presumptuous to the disciples. Please, don't miss this point. When you understand this as the context, reading Luke's account of Jesus' instructions on prayer has a different outcome than what you have seen before. I want you to read what Jesus says right after He teaches the disciples how to pray:

> *And he said to them, "Which of you who has a friend will go to him at midnight and say to him, 'Friend, lend me three loaves, for a friend of mine has arrived on a journey, and I have nothing to set before him'; and he will answer from within, 'Do not bother me; the door is now shut, and my children are with me in bed. I cannot get up and give you anything'? I tell you, though he will not get up and give him anything because he is his friend, yet because of his impudence he will rise and give him whatever he needs. And I tell you, ask, and it will be given to you; seek, and you will find; knock, and it will be opened to you. For everyone who asks receives, and the one who seeks finds, and to the one who knocks it will be opened.*

What father among you, if his son asks for a fish, will instead of a fish give him a serpent; or if he asks for an egg, will give him a scorpion? If you then, who are evil, know how to give good gifts to your children, how much more will the heavenly Father give the Holy Spirit to those who ask him!" (Luke 11:5-13)

Persistence! God answers the prayers of the persistent, right? Answer to prayer is simply a matter of willpower. Don't give up on prayer and God won't give up on you! This is what we have been taught by modern evangelicalism for the last hundred years. It is not only wrong, but damaging to the actual purpose of prayer. Jesus is not calling the disciples over to show them how persistence will get more answers to prayer. He is exposing their hearts to the safe access they have in calling God their "Father." Remember, they had never seen anyone approach God in this way in the past. No one had ever approached declaring sonship as his right of access. Jesus gives the disciples brief but powerful examples to bring this foreign concept into reality. In prayer, they are to approach the Father with boldness as a son would to an affectionate father. But this isn't just for the sake of praise and worship. They actually are encouraged to make requests of their Father believing He eagerly waits to answer. Now, reread verse 8 and ask yourself, *Is Luke talking about the man knocking at the door, or the man inside the house?* Jesus said, "I tell you, though he will not get up and give him anything because he is his friend, yet because of his impudence he will rise and give him whatever he needs." The man answers the requests because of *his* (the man in the house) impudence, not because of the neighbor knocking. The question we must answer is, what is impudence?

The word *anaideia* can mean "avoidance of shame." While it did come to have the meaning of "persistence," the concept of shame was linked with it in the first century. The parable would thus mean that just as the man in bed would respond so as not to incur shame (for having refused the needs of a visitor to his community), so God will always do what is honorable and consistent with His character.

So what is Jesus' point in the story? If God said He would answer, He will keep His word. The reputation of God is placed as the guarantee. Jesus was showing the disciples that this new access to God could be trusted. God will always respond to what is consistent with His character. This is why he concludes by saying, "If you then, who are evil, know how to give good gifts to your children, how much more will the heavenly Father give the Holy Spirit to those who ask him!"

The access granted to the disciples was so foreign to their religious experience, Jesus had to assure them through multiple illustrations that this access was trustworthy. Calvin wrote:

> *"Whenever we engage in prayer, there are two things*
> *to be considered, both that we may have access to God,*
> *and that we may rely on Him with full and unshaken*

confidence: his fatherly love toward us, and His boundless power. Let us therefore entertain no doubt, that God is willing to receive us graciously, that He is ready to listen to our prayers." (Commentary on a Harmony of the Evangelists, John Calvin)

Calvin's point is that the answers to our prayers are given not because of our persistence, but our position as a child. We have confidence God will hear and answer because of who we are to Him—an adopted child. The *Westminster Larger Catechism, Question 189* says: "The preface of the Lord's Prayer…teacheth us, when we pray, to draw near to God with confidence of His fatherly goodness, and our interest therein; with reverence, and all other childlike dispositions, heavenly affections, and due apprehensions of his sovereign power, majesty, and gracious condescension."

Jesus is holding out His hand toward the disciples and calling them to stand next to Him: "You have the same right as I do to call Him Father. Come here, tell Him what you need." Jesus teaches His disciples that they have access to the very God they are called to fear and reverence in the Torah. They can and should approach Him as their Father. They have every right to depend on Him for everything in life and make requests as they are needed. This brings us back to our original question—what about answers to prayer?

Here is the catch: Jesus didn't, nor does the rest of the Bible, give us freedom in our requests. We have been told that we can request anything we want. Think of a request, ask for it, and wait for the answer. When it doesn't come, that's your fault for not having enough faith. According to the prayer that Jesus set before the disciples, the key to all of it was the one parameter that was set: God's will (Matthew 6:10). We approach God on His terms to accomplish His will. Jesus is telling the disciples that you can ask God for anything that relates to His will being done. *Anything*, and He will give it to you. In other words, Jesus set the parameters for our requests. We don't come to God on the behalf of our desires but in light of His. He promises to answer prayers that align with His will. To some, this sounds less enticing than asking for whatever we desire. It sounds better that God would pull out His magic wand and sprinkle fairy dust on all of our pumpkins, making them into our next best story to tell all of our Christian friends. Wouldn't it give Him more glory for me to tell a story about the miracle He provided than simply praying that His will be done? Let me point us back to the purpose of prayer. Prayer is admitting our dependence on God alone for everything. The Lord's Prayer perfectly explains that we ask God for what sustains us (metaphor seen in our daily bread), where we find forgiveness (forgive us our debts), and what guides us (lead us not into temptation). When we make requests of God to provide these necessities, He will answer them if we are asking according to the parameters given to us by Jesus.

I don't want to oversimplify prayer, because as we can see, prayer is still a mystery. Even in Jesus' teaching there still remains mystery. My point is that we must adjust our mindset to approach God according to His revealed will instead of throwing up spiritual lottery tickets hoping one lands in the answer pot. What is the will of God? Redemption. The more I embrace a reformed perspective, the story of the Bible becomes more and more clarifying as it relates to topics like prayer. If the purpose of the Bible is to tell the story of God's redemption of sinners, it would seem logical to conclude that God's will on earth is redeeming sinners. To pray according to the will of God then would be to pray for the accomplishment of redemption. Ask for whatever you need (as it relates to My will), and I will give it to you. If our focus should be the accomplishment of redemption, how would this change our requests? Our focus is on what God is accomplishing, not on what we are attempting to accomplish. Our question to the Father should be; *Does my request align with your redemption?* Healing for a loved one, a new job, travel safety, or courage to share your faith should all be with the perspective of redemption in mind. God will accomplish His will. He is allowing us to participate in this amazing plan. As we are used by God, He calls us to make the needed requests to sustain us in this life. What a glorious thought. We have everything we need to participate in the accomplishment of His will. Does God need us to participate? Of course not. He needs nothing. He graciously brings us along to witness His glory in action. We bring Him glory by trusting by faith in His redemption, and taking this good news to the world.

Conclusion

If you skipped this chapter to read my conclusion, I get it. *He's probably just giving me what I've already heard before about how I need to pray more.* I feel your pain. The lack of prayer in most Christians is the result of confusion, unanswered requests, and pietism. We want the blessings of God, so we use prayer to position ourselves to receive them. Living in a constant state of guilt is likened to constantly feeling like you are on the verge of drowning. You only have enough energy to keep your head above water, but never enough to enjoy a relaxing swim. You can't even remember the last time you enjoyed praying unless it was for the steak dinner last week. Enjoying prayer is not about systems, persistence, positions, or disciplines. To enjoy prayer you need to exchange your current reality for another, and move from a pietistic world into a confessional world. We don't earn the right to spend time with our Father, it has been granted to us. We don't maintain the right to be with Him, He guaranteed our access through Christ. This is the difference between living under the pressure of pietism and in the joy of the confessions. We approach prayer from the status of what has been done for us instead of what we must do.

Try it now; just let your heart bleed out to your Father. Are you scared of what He might think if you say what you are really feeling? Well, He already knows. You see, unlike your earthly father, you can't hide what's really going on. Might as well lean over onto His armchair and rest in His presence. Confess your lack of faith, desire, ability to fight sin. Seek the forgiveness He promises to give you. Ask Him to increase your faith, boldness, and love for others. Ask Him without placing some sort of requirement on yourself. Don't promise to try harder. Don't promise you will do better next time. Stop bargaining with God. You're a beggar who the Father adopted and now calls "My child." He promised to provide everything you need to accomplish the mission He gave you to love Him and love others. He calls us to simply depend on Him for it through prayer. He has given you everything you need to play your part in His mission to find His lost sheep—simply ask for it. It's His will that you depend on Him and that you talk to Him. He wants to hear about everything. Praises. Worship. Pain. Joy. Defeat. Victory. Everything. Because He loves you. That is the picture of love. Jesus demonstrated this kind of approach to the Father as well. In the garden, Jesus cried out in pain to His Father because it was almost too much for Him to bear. He cried. He wept. He shared His pain. If we depend on our Father to save us from His wrath and bring us home, we can trust His words when He says He will listen and answer our requests according to His will. We are saved according to His will, we seek answers according to His will, and our experience on this earth will be ten times more enjoyable with the Father in prayer than without.

My prayer for you today is that through all of your doubt, fatigue, pain, and struggle, you would lift your eyes to see the glory of God in the face of Jesus Christ. God's love for you is not dependent upon your performance. God set His love on you while you were a sinner. God accepts you now as His child because of what His Son, Jesus Christ, did on your behalf. You are righteous, according to the ledger books! You didn't earn it. You can't maintain it. You can't lose it. You simply enjoy the benefits of being declared righteous.

You have every right at any moment to run to our Father and speak your mind. Moments of pure joy expressing His greatness. Tear-filled cries complaining of sin's demands on your broken body. Requests for help. Every word that falls from your lips, the Father holds as precious in His hand—because you are precious in His sight.

The joy of the Lord is your strength today! Rest your heart in the promise that He is pleased with you, that He loves you, and that He will protect you. When we rest, obedience becomes our joy and not our dread. We see glorifying our Father to be a worthy effort, not means of earning favor. Rest, weary saint. Rest and look to Christ today. You may not feel it, you will never fully understand it, but you belong to God. You are His child, and He loves you. What a gift prayer is to the weary pilgrim!